A New Era in
Inventory Management
for the Distribution Industry

Copyright© 1993 Charles J. Bodenstab

Published in the United States by
Hilta Press, Minneapolis, Minnesota

ISBN 0-9639358-0-1

First printing 1993

Charles J. Bodenstab
2607 W. Lafayette Road
Excelsior, Minnesota 55331

A New Era in
Inventory Management
for the Distribution Industry

by

Charles J. Bodenstab

Design and Illustrations by
Cucci Design

HILTA
PRESS

Dedication

To those who are so special in my heart:
to my wife Pamela,
my children, and their families.

Contents

Section One

Tools and Rules for Inventory Management

Section Two

Computer-Aided Inventory Management System "Demand Forecasting"

Acknowledgments

I would like to acknowledge the always good advice and editing of one of the world's true gentlemen, Bob Stoll. Also, within the Data Systems & Management organization, my manuscript benefited from the review and editing by some really fine people – Matt Rauh, Bob Tuttle, Tom Dietsche and Dan Bjorkman.

Additionally, I would like to express appreciation for the editing, guidance, and sound advice I received from Evelyn Vida of Johnston Design Office.

Ultimately, I owe a debt of gratitude to the many people I had the privilege of directing during the past forty years. So much of what I have learned about business and operations in general came from these talented, wise people. They may have been reporting to me, but I was learning what it was all about from them!

1.0   Introduction

With effective management and planning, you can down-size your inventory by 20%, improve your order fill rate, and free up working capital.

A tremendous portion of the capital base of this country — almost $200 billion — is tied up in inventory. My experience is that 20 percent of this inventory could be eliminated, and the effectiveness and utility of the remainder could be significantly improved. In this book, I offer some new approaches to inventory management that can help you downsize your inventories and make them work for you.

In the past decade, inventories have generally gotten unfavorable press. We business people have been inundated by a regular chant: "Inventories are bad!" JIT (just in time) preaches that inventories should be ruthlessly eliminated and product should arrive "just in time" to be processed and used. As with most management fads, the issue is more complex, however. Inventory *can* perform a major positive function by trading off various elements of cost and performance. In other words, inventory can be good!

We should classify as "bad," inventory that is being used to compensate for bad management or bad planning. We should also classify as "bad," inventory that is simply ineffective in its composition and therefore fails to perform its intended function.

Inventory can act as a substitute for a higher-cost alternative. By having inventory, we can ship in more economic truck loads, we can buffer the manufacturing process against interruption, and we can provide immediate service to our customers (so that they can practice JIT).

A recent article in the *New York Times*

reported that much of the downtown traffic congestion in Tokyo can be attributed to many vehicles making small, inefficient deliveries. The Tokyo traffic would probably improve if Japanese businesses would carry larger inventories, and restock less frequently and in larger quantities.

Too many of our inventories are out of balance and improperly structured. Inventory management is all too often relegated to the "back room" of management. It certainly does not get a fraction of the management attention given to sales and marketing. Aside from inventory's lack of glamour, management hasn't been sure what it could do to improve this area. Besides, it's grungy work, requiring a lot of number pushing and taking a lot of time. The fact that inventory is the "guts" of the business seems to have been overlooked.

When it comes to business management, we are in many ways like the man who trips and spills his change on the front lawn, but goes into the living room to look for it because "the light is better." Similarly, we tend to put our management emphasis where "the light is better," and shy away from areas such as inventory management where the ability to make a contribution is more obscure.

The problem is further compounded by the fact that the tools available in the area of inventory management have been rather primitive. Until recently, computer software gave managers little more than rough printouts of past history plus on-hand balances. Even then, the information was poorly organized. It was common to see sales history stated as "current month" and "year to date," with no trend data month by month and no processed forecast.

Gradually, computer systems are becoming more sophisticated and are providing organized information that truly facilitates inventory management. Many systems have been influenced by Gordon Graham, who has written two inventory management books that deal with a tremendous range of inventory issues. I have some major differences of opinion with Graham regarding the specific process of building a restocking order, but nevertheless hold many of his other principles in high regard.

The software systems that follow Graham's concepts have at least brought some quantitative organized structure to the process. I feel we have made another quantum step ahead with the system I'm introducing in this book.

Historical Perspective

Before going any further, it may be helpful to give you some idea of my background. During the 1950s and early 1960s, I gained considerable experience in the Management Information Systems field including work in developing some of the earliest quantitative approaches to inventory management. This was followed by a string of positions in line management most of which were as General Manager of fairly large divisions in the $250 million range.

In 1983, I acquired Battery and Tire Warehouse, an automotive distributorship in Minnesota, and entered the world of small business. The company was supposed to be moderately profitable, but was, in fact, hemorrhaging. Inventory was one of the key disaster areas. It took almost two years and a series of 80-hour weeks to clean up the operation.

Actually, within the first year we became profitable, but that resulted in part from some good luck. Minnesota had a record cold winter which greatly increased the demand for batteries. Though luck played a role in our success, if our inventory hadn't been cleaned up by the time the cold snap hit, we would not have been able to capitalize on the stroke of good fortune.

Inventory was a disaster area in the business I acquired. It took time to implement an inventory management system, but it really paid off!

It was during this period that many of the concepts and ideas discussed in this book were developed and refined. My involvement in the real world of small business insured that the ideas which had been developed in big business environments were effectively restructured for the small businessman.

As I struggled to implement inventory management systems at Battery and Tire Warehouse, it became clear to me that theoretical statisticians had completely missed the reality of the typical distributor. This failure to deal with the real world issues of the distributor delayed the introduction of more sophisticated systems into inventory management in general. Distributors quickly discovered that while the statistical theory was technically sound, it didn't work in their situation because theoreticians had not taken into account the unique conditions under which distributors operate.

As a final postscript to the Battery and Tire Warehouse acquisition, I sold the company in late 1992, just about ten years after I purchased it. The company was sold at a considerable premium, over twenty times earnings, which was possible, in part, because innovative inventory management had significantly contributed to the underlying strength of the company.

This book is not intended to be a comprehensive review of every aspect of inventory control. It would take volumes to cover the many facets of the day-to-day workings of inventory control and management. Moreover, since each company has its own unique challenges and problems, there are no universal solutions. Consequently, I have chosen to highlight a series of areas in inventory management that seem to be routinely mishandled and where some major pay-off opportunities exist. I focus on the areas that are critical in taking a company from a rudimentary form of inventory control to an advanced position of inventory management.

The book is organized into two sections. The first is a discussion of the non-technical aspects of inventory control. Again, it is by no means a comprehensive discussion of all the tools and rules of inventory management. Rather, I focus on areas of inventory control where I have seen the greatest mistakes. Until these areas are identified and cleaned up, it is impossible to take advantage of the exciting computer tools and systems now available.

The second part of the book introduces some very unique computer-oriented techniques for effectively managing inventory.

Enough of the generalitics. Let's get into the specifics!

Potential Benefits

For just about every distributor, gross margins have been under constant pressure for the past two decades. In my own industry of automotive parts and accessories, 35 percent gross margins were par for the course 20 years ago. Now 20 percent is more common, and much business is transacted well below this level. The distributors who have responded to this pressure with cost reductions and better overall management have survived; the ones who couldn't have simply gone under. In fact, during the past ten years over 80,000 distributors have disappeared from the national scene.

Ironically, there were major upward pressures on costs during the very period in which distributors had to cut costs to survive the reduced margins. The hyper inflation of the 70s, increased hospitalization costs of the 80s, and taxes of all types drove up operating costs. The implications were clear. Operating costs had to be reduced in other areas to offset the slew of rising expenses.

Rising operating costs can be effectively offset by efficient inventory management.

One key area of opportunity for cost reduction is in the more efficient management of inventory. The potential returns in this area are staggering.

There is no one theoretically ideal inventory level common to all business. The relationship of inventory size to sales is complex and different for each industry and, for that matter, each distributor. Customer expectations, the number of direct shipments, the existence of some retail trade, and many other factors have an impact on the fundamental relationship of inventory to sales.

Nevertheless, inventory reductions of 20 percent are not unreasonable, if attacked with the concepts that we will be discussing throughout this book. This savings can even be coupled with a simultaneous improvement in order fill rates. Obviously the benefits will vary with the individual and the current degree of inventory savvy being used. Still, these levels of improvements are possible even if the savvy is relatively high but the guidance being used is from the typical primitive computerized inventory control system.

Assume a business does $10 million in sales, has an inventory of $1.8 million, and has a before-tax profit of $150,000. If that company can reduce its inventory by 20 percent — that's $360,000 in cash — that in turn is worth at least $36,000 a year in added profits due to reduced borrowing alone. Add to that at least another $36,000 due to reduced obsolescence, insurance, space, taxes, and handling, and profits have improved by 50 percent. We are not through. Improved fill rates will strengthen the competitive position of the business, and the actual manual time and cost of managing the inventory will be slashed!

My company provides an excellent example of the potential in labor savings alone. At Battery and Tire Warehouse, we had three product managers over the three key product areas of batteries, tires, and accessories.

The product manager for batteries retired a few years ago and we simply didn't replace him. With the aid of our computer systems, the job was no longer intensely time consuming. I was able to do the battery reordering in my spare time, since I could prepare a restocking order for a major vendor in 15 minutes or less. This order tracked trends and seasonality, worried about economic break points, considered pallet requirements, balanced to a full truck load, and, finally, allowed for considerable human interaction that drew on my subjective knowledge which was outside the computer's realm. Moreover, the decision process that determined what product should be ordered and in what amount was unrivaled in thoroughness, accuracy, and speed.

Although the labor savings was nice, the real payoff was in outright inventory reduction and improvement in order fill rates. We went from four turns to seven turns in the very first year and were at ten turns by the time I sold my business. Concurrently, we went from a fill rate of about 85 percent to over 95 percent.

Some Comments Regarding "Simplicity"

There is a school of thought that flatly states that you should stay away from any system that utilizes calculations that cannot be reproduced manually on the back of an envelope by a non-technical person. The feeling is that unless people can manually reproduce what a computer is doing, they will be unwilling to utilize the system.

Upon reflection, I believe that people really do not care any more about the complexity of what is going on inside a machine. We have long since given up on our ability to track the full technology of the systems we employ in today's world. What people *do want*, however, are systems that both work and are *simple to use*. In order to enjoy the benefits of new technology, we have accepted the fact that sophisticated systems have outrun our capability to trace their full methodology.

Ironically, the proponents of "simplicity" use systems that are, in fact, complex to implement and operate. In their avoidance of "complex" techniques, they come up with a tremendous variety of manual steps and actions that make it difficult to keep all the steps straight. It becomes a case of being "put to death by a thousand small cuts."

Simple computer programs can be difficult to operate; complex computer programs can be simple to operate.

Let me restate the idea in an analogy. A model T Ford is a tremendously "simple" car, particularly when compared with a modern Escort. The engine is the essence of simplicity, as is the entire drive train. With the least amount of mechanical skills you can repair even the larger items.

On the other hand, if you have ever driven a Model T, as I am afraid I must admit I have, then you know that it is very difficult and "complex" to drive. You have to manually advance the spark with speed, you have to manually adjust the choke with engine temperature, and you have to double clutch the shift under certain circumstances.

The new Escort is a very "complex" car. I shudder when I look at what is under the hood. Yet, the Escort is a very simple car to operate as compared to the Model T. All the previously required manual interventions happen automatically, to say nothing of many functions that the Model T designers never even dreamed possible.

This is analogous to the concept we want to develop with our inventory system. We may incorporate some complex techniques, but as long as they happen automatically and do the job for which they are designed, we end up with the best of both worlds.

The other key point that proponents of "simplicity" make is that unless the individuals doing the inventory control understand the inner workings of the system, they will not use it. Interesting! Can you see a situation where a production worker tells management, "I really do not understand the full technology of the high precision, numerically controlled laser torch that you just installed, so I am going to continue to use my old mechanical saw."

Of course you can't imagine this happening. Production workers do not often understand the inner technology of the sophisticated equipment they are charged to use. But they do know how to operate the equipment in an intelligent and effective manner by interacting with the external controls of the system.

Why do we buy into this idea that people in the inventory control area can arbitrarily sabotage something that has a far greater potential benefit to the company than even one of the more elaborate pieces of production equipment? The reason ties back into the history of inventory management.

An aura of mystique has surrounded this area as the inventory practitioners have applied their used Ouija boards to periodically come up with replenishment orders. In fairness to the practitioners, they had little choice, since there were no adequate systems to give them guidance and support. Unfortunately this mystique then fed on itself, and the practitioners took on the mantle of high priests with their own special kingdoms. To make matters worse, business writers of the time then perpetuated this absurdity by implying that we have to compromise our methodology to cater to this state of affairs.

Frankly, management *cannot* accept this situation and must take an attitude that the inventory control function will move into the modern age, technology and all. We can't be intimidated by this function any more than we are intimidated by production workers who, incidentally, had their own brand of black magic as it related to the earlier pieces of production equipment.

Business managers do have a bona fide concern about the more sophisticated statistical techniques that will be discussed in this book. Will they work in the real world of business? The unfortunate truth about these techniques is that they have not always worked in the business environment.

What I have done, after considerable refinement and testing under true operating conditions is create a system that captures the power of classical statistical techniques, but contains numerous modifiers that compensate for their flaws. The net effect is a system that has a sound theoretical basis, but which functions extremely well in the less-than-perfect world of the distributor. Additionally, it is a system that, while "complex" internally, is actually very simple to operate. Finally, the system de-mystifies the inventory replenishment process and allows someone who is not intimately familiar with the product line to efficiently produce a replenishment order.

The proof that we had achieved our goal of de-mystifying the reorder process was demonstrated some years ago at Battery and Tire Warehouse when our product manager of accessory products was called to serve in Desert Storm. He handled the reordering of products for over sixty vendors. Without our computerized inventory system we would have had a catastrophe on our hands. As it was, we were able to pick up his duties with a minimum of crises. Were our replenishment orders as good as his? Not completely, since he had certain background that we missed, but we were very close and little was lost.

By the time you finish the inventory reordering part of this book, you will see how a computer system can de-mystify the reordering process for you.

Tools and Rules
for
Inventory Management

General Comments   1.0

First, I want to cover some aspects of inventory management that have nothing to do with computers. These tools and rules are crucial for inventory control and can ultimately have as much impact on inventory effectiveness as the computer. Moreover, when these aspects of inventory management are under control, the foundation is strong for the eventual application of computer systems.

This section will deal with a number of tools that seem to be habitually misused and with rules that seem to be habitually violated by many distributors, and which — given a bit of attention — can yield significant benefits.

Let me admit up front that we will be covering some fairly unsophisticated and straightforward concepts. This is not high tech stuff. Nevertheless, these areas of inventory management seem to get neglected at many companies and are ripe for corrective action.

The Authorized Stock List

Every distributor should have an established, published "Authorized Stock List." This is a list that states what items you have in stock or are committing to supply to customers upon demand. Items should be added to and deleted from this list in some organized manner. Based upon demand, some items you carry may not appear on your authorized list, with the understanding that they may be special ordered with some lead time for availability.

A stock list is a fundamental operations tool, yet I am amazed at how many companies have a fuzzy, ill-structured approach to stock lists. When I took over my own firm, it was interesting to find that there were items that we "sort of" stocked. Sort of? How does one "sort of" stock something?

I do some consulting work on the side, and as part of this effort I was working with a company to bring its inventories under control and to free up some badly needed cash. The first thing we did was instruct the sales and marketing group to establish an authorized inventory list which, until then, was non-existent. This simple act clarified the whole relationship between the manufacturing and marketing functions, to say nothing of the new image created with the customers. If we had stopped at this point and made no other changes, there would have been a significant favorable impact on the organization.

In some companies, the stock list may actually include the entire product line, covering 100 percent of the items. This is fairly rare, however, and the more typical situation is that you will attempt to stock to the classic situation where 20 percent of the items cover 80 percent of the demand. This figure can swing all the way from 30-70 to 10-90 depending on the industry and market.

Determining which items belong in that 20 percent group is easier said than done. If you had a year's worth of demand data in the computer for all your customers' inquiries, you would be in great shape. You would then be able to sort the list, and the classic pattern would stand out sharply. Unfortunately, it is a rare company that has this type of data, so we have to resort to other methods.

In any established company, there is usually some formal or even informal awareness of what items the company stocks. It may be fuzzy and unpublished, but it is a beginning. From this starting point, it becomes a matter of adding and deleting items over time to strengthen and refine the list until it approximates the classic situation.

Determining which items to delete from the list is relatively easy, particularly if you have a fairly decent computer system. Periodically, you should get a printout of stock items, identify the items that have not shown more than X movements in Y time period, and then make a management decision to drop the items from your authorized list.

Adding items is a bit trickier. In some companies, all customer demands, stocked and non-stocked, are recorded in the computer and periodically analyzed for their popularity. This approach is very comprehensive and certainly provides excellent guidance for keeping the list current and effective.

Unfortunately, in most companies, capturing information of this nature is not very practical. The volume of information can be overwhelming, and since its only use is for adding items to the stock list, it's a questionable return on the investment. Moreover, the accuracy of the information is often in doubt, since the data does not get used in a way that forces disciplined data entry. (In contrast to stocked items, where a bad part number has major repercussions.)

At Battery and Tire Warehouse, we handled this issue of adding items in a subjective way. We had a form that anyone could use to initiate the addition of a specific SKU (Stock Keeping Unit). The initiative could come from a salesperson, a manufacturer's rep, a product manager, our order entry desk, or anyone who had some valid reason to believe an item warranted addition to our authorized stock list. The form, which contained some comment on the rationale for stocking the item, was reviewed and approved by the associated product manager and me; then the item was formally added to the list.

Incidentally, not every item approved and added turns out to be a winner. It is not at all uncommon to have 10 to 20 percent of the items we added to our list pulled a year or two later. If you are rigorous in pulling items when they do not pan out, and if you do not stock large quantities immediately, then this is not a particularly painful process. Besides, unless you are willing to risk, you will unduly inhibit the process of adding items.

One argument that develops in this area of stocking covers the "alleged" need to keep a lot of slow-moving product on hand because the customer expects it, and won't buy the popular stuff from you unless you can also supply the slow-moving items. There is some truth to this point, but generally the concept is used to justify stocking far more items than are warranted.

Generally, in every business there is an individual (it may even be you) who is defending a list of about 30 slow-moving items of a single vendor, based on the "customer expectation rationale." Ironically, it is most likely accepted that the company shouldn't stock everything available. The items being defended, therefore, are usually some that just happen to be in your inventory, and have no more logic to being stocked than the hundreds that move with the same infrequency, but are not stocked. The point is to be consistent. Once you agree that you are not going to stock everything and are going to stock only the items that have a respectable return on their inventory investment, then stick to your policy.

I want to interject a point here about the ABC concept of stocking. This is the classical theory that puts product into three classes: A, B, and C, with the idea of dealing differently with each class, due to its profitability or its critical nature. In practice, "A items" would be given a higher level of safety stock so that their fill rates would be very high. "B items" would be given a lower safety stock, resulting in a lower fill rate. The net result, in theory, is that you would be putting your resources where the greatest payoff exists. Most advanced computer software systems have provisions for this ABC classification concept.

In my opinion, while the concept is sound in theory, it is not sound in the real world of the distributor. My customers, for example, couldn't care less whether I make 10, 20, or 25 percent gross margin on a particular SKU. If I deliberately starve the inventory on a "C item" that makes only 12 percent gross margin, and I am excessively out of stock on that item or that class of items, my customer may become extremely unhappy with me as a supplier and may drop me and all my "A items" in the process.

When you establish an authorized stock list, it becomes, in effect, a contract with your customers. You are stating that you are going to routinely stock these items, and that you are going to have these products on hand 95 or 97 percent of the time, regardless of their gross margin levels.

Let's summarize:

- Have a definite, published, formal list of the products you routinely inventory.
- Have a rigorous, structured program for adding and deleting items.
- Be consistent in your rationale for stocking items.

Ruthlessly eliminate slow-moving or distressed product. The operative word here is "ruthlessly." This product, by definition, is not going to move itself. Additionally, your sales force is not going to voluntarily move it. Salespeople want to sell new product and not bother with distressed product. Management must drive on this issue; it is a management area of responsibility.

Slow-moving and distressed merchandise not only ties up capital, it has a negative, corrosive effect on the system. It ties up space and undermines housekeeping. For every month product sits in your inventory, it costs you a minimum of one percent due to the cost of funds alone. Consequently, if you sell something after it has sat in your inventory for 18 months, you would have been ahead if you had dumped it out earlier for 20 percent less.

The retail trade, particularly in women's clothing, is only too aware of this issue. Note how retailers ruthlessly cut prices on product that is out of season or out of fashion in order to get it out of the store. Discounts of 20 to 80 percent are not a problem for these retailers. They realize the disastrous impact a steady accumulation of this product has on the system.

In the hard goods area, we do not seem to have the same awareness. We take the attitude that the shelf life for our products is good and — who knows — someone may want that item tomorrow. Yet, for every time you were able to sell off these slow-moving items and obtain full price, you paid a tremendous price in carrying costs and warehouse obstruction from the items that didn't sell.

Getting rid of slow-moving product is a pain. The first year I had Battery and Tire Warehouse, we dropped our inventories from $1.5 million to $1.1, while our sales increased from $7.0 million to $10.0. Our new controls and computer system insured that we were not generating more slow-moving inventory, but a good part of that $400,000 inventory drop was slow-moving product, and it definitely didn't go away by itself. We ended up using at least a dozen techniques to move it out of the system.

Many of the methods we used were fairly common. We ran specials at heavy discounts. We substituted wherever possible. We provided the sales force with printed lists to highlight the availability of these items. With a tear in our eye, we even threw product into the dumpster.

We also worked hard at forcing our vendors to accept product returns for credit. Ironically, a new vendor will often do a "stock lift" of his competition's product to gain entry, but an existing vendor will show little interest in taking back his own distressed product. We threatened, cajoled, pleaded, and did everything else we could to get our vendors to help us in this major clean-up task. By having our story together, and having our support data quantitatively displayed, we were quite successful in this effort.

Another technique we used was to lean hard on the sales force. In the early days we used some spiffs with the sales force and order desk for their help. Later, I periodically prepared lists of product we wanted to move, and informed the sales force that it was a "condition of employment" that they move at least 50 items off the list in the next 60 days. You would be surprised at what they were capable of selling.

Let's summarize:

- Ruthlessly eliminate slow-moving and distressed merchandise.

- Provide your employees with incentives and management leadership to get the job done.

- Resist the temptation to hang on to product on the outside chance that it will be needed shortly. Some will, but overall you are fooling yourself.

One of the most important factors in driving down inventory levels while improving order fill rates is the frequency of placing restocking orders. Believe it or not, order frequency is much more important than lead time, which tends to get the greater amount of attention.

If you have two choices, one where the order frequency is weekly and the lead time is four weeks, and another where the order frequency is four weeks and the lead time is one week, the first would be best.

If you can order frequently, even with long lead times, the bulk of the product is in the "pipeline." This is to your financial advantage, since you do not incur the cost of inventory until it arrives.

Let's take an extreme example. Assume that you could order every day, and the lead time is three weeks. Three weeks sounds like a real problem, but just think of what would take place. You would have 15 orders at various stages in the pipeline. As product went out the door, deliveries would be arriving every day for replenishment.

I had a practical example of this situation at Battery and Tire Warehouse. After we got our inventory control system up and running, the salesmen came to me with great concern. We were ordering batteries from our primary supplier every three working days since we were able to generate a full truck load in that time. In the past, we had been ordering three and four truck loads every few weeks. The lead time from the supplier was two weeks.

Their comment was, "Charlie, we're in trouble! There aren't any batteries in the warehouse, and in this business unless you have full shelves you simply aren't going to sell batteries." I asked about their back-orders. They told me their back-orders were virtually non-existent, but that it didn't make any difference. "You have to have a lot of inventory to sell batteries."

What they didn't grasp was that product was flowing in every three days and, furthermore, we actually had a lot of inventory. It simply wasn't in our warehouse and on our books. It was on our vendors' books. Additionally, if we were out of an item, it was usually for only a few days, in contrast to the past, when an item would be out of stock for weeks.

Incidentally, all this theory is based on the fact that you have a respectable forecasting system and inventory control program. But that is exactly what we will be developing as we go forward.

Okay, we may agree that frequent reordering is desirable, but we also realize that there are a number of factors that determine how frequently you can trigger a restocking order, many of which are outside your control. Most vendors have minimum order quantities that must be met to earn the most favorable price or to have the product shipped prepaid. Consequently, your sales volume for that vendor will generally establish how frequently your sales generate a restock that meets the minimum ship level.

As a simple illustration, if a full truckload of product is 30,000 pounds and you sell roughly 60,000 pounds of that product per month, then you should be able to generate a restock about every two weeks. The key point regarding this example is that you should order one truckload every two weeks, and not two loads once per month.

Without a computerized inventory system, the task of building a reorder is often quite formidable or, at best, awkward. The process can take literally hours, and consequently you may feel that you simply do not have the luxury of placing frequent orders. In the second section of this book, we will be introducing concepts whereby the computer assumes this time-consuming burden. But even if you are saddled with a cumbersome system for generating a reorder, frequent reordering is valid, and worth considerable effort to achieve.

In the second section of this book, we will also discuss at length the issue of reorder frequency, since the computer system takes this variable into account in building a reorder. Yet even in the computer environment, unless the purchasing manager orders as frequently as the economics allow, the full advantages of the system will not be realized.

Incidentally, there is one extra benefit of this policy. You will be able to place orders for non-stocked items more frequently, thereby being more responsive to customer needs for the slower-moving product.

Let's summarize:

- Take the time and trouble to order as frequently as the economics will allow.

- Do not yield to the impulse to save time by combining orders.

For reasons that are difficult to fathom, there is a tendency to order fairly substantial amounts of a new SKU. Granted, there will be times when this practice is perfectly justifiable, such as when the item is needed by a specific new account and his demand levels are known in advance. Our concern is related to the other situation where there is no prior pattern, but sufficient evidence has accumulated that says this item looks like a reasonable candidate for stocking.

In this situation, there seems to be a normal tendency to order a larger quantity than is justified. What is wrong with ordering "two" or "four" of an item, rather than "a pallet load?" Then as demand materializes, the system that we will be creating will do a wonderful job of bringing in the right replenishment amounts.

Ironically, I am as susceptible to this tendency to overstock a new item as the next person. One of our battery suppliers came out with a new innovative battery called the "Switch," which allowed you to switch over to an unused energy reserve in the battery if you had left your lights on. It came in two group sizes, and damned if I didn't order a pallet of 40 each as an initial order. The concept was a flop, and a year later I was dumping most of those batteries at distressed prices. What was wrong with ordering six of each, and then when they went out, ordering more in the next reorder?

I was able to trace a lot of the dead stock I inherited at Battery and Tire Warehouse to this tendency. Time and time again they would order large amounts of a new item as if it had been selling like gangbusters. Typically, we were sitting with 22 of an item, left over from an initial order of a pallet of 24.

Maybe you are immune to this virus, but I have seen the symptoms all too often.

Let's summarize:

- If possible, order relatively small amounts of a new SKU being added to the authorized inventory list.

- Then as sales develop, reorder more.

On occasion an opportunity will arise to purchase someone's inventory at extremely attractive prices. It may be a company going out of business or dropping a particular product line; it may be a vendor unloading inventory. In any case, the situation is tremendously seductive when you are looking at discounts of 20 to 80 percent.

I am not saying you should never pursue these opportunities, but I am saying that you should be very cautious. Probably a high percentage of the product is slow-moving or distressed. You might realize a quick killing by selling off the "good stuff," but most likely the residue will either sit around, or you will consume a fair amount of resources getting rid of it.

In my business, tire manufacturers will periodically offer truckloads of "blems." This product, which is perfectly fine except for some cosmetic problems, is offered to us at 20 percent off the normal price. Our salesmen love blems, since they can play hero to their customers, and it gives them a momentary advantage in the marketplace.

The problem with blems is that we have to take the truckload with the manufacturer's mix of product, not what our reorder system is calling for. The net effect is that 80 percent of the "good stuff" is sold overnight, and the remainder sits around and grows whiskers if we let it. Don't get me wrong, I do periodically go for the blem loads, but I watch it carefully and keep after the sales people to get rid of the remainder.

Incidentally, I have seen tire distributors whose practice of going after deals was a contributing factor in their demise. They ended up with a tremendous amount of inventory that was on the books at full price but, in fact, was the residue of past "deals." The operating statements and balance sheets looked fine, but more and more cash was being tied up in this residue inventory to the point where it simply brought the company to its knees.

Let's summarize:

- Be extremely cautious about opportunities to buy what are, in effect, someone else's problems.
- Recognize that only a fraction of the goods will move at the inflated gross margins; the reminder will become cash-consuming residue.

Have very good housekeeping in your warehouse. This is not a particularly profound point, but is nevertheless extremely important. Frankly, I am appalled by the abominable lack of housekeeping I see at numerous warehouses. Aisles are cluttered, product is stacked randomly, over-stocked items are strewn wherever, product and shelves are dirty, lighting is poor, bins are not identified — the list goes on and on. We all know what good housekeeping is. The key is to do it!

When I acquired Battery and Tire Warehouse, we had the same situation that I am describing, and it contributed to our problems. Product often couldn't be located. Product was damaged or became dirty. Product existed, but was reordered on the mistaken assumption that we were out.

We did a major cleanup, and again it was management's responsibility to take the lead. It didn't take a lot of time or money to get things looking great.

Early in the effort, I was on the other side of an aisle and overheard two of my warehousemen negatively commenting on my cleanup efforts. They thought it was going to be just a matter of time before I realized we were an automotive warehouse and not a supermarket. I didn't confront them, but made an even stronger resolve to achieve my housekeeping objectives.

An interesting thing occurred. Once the place was straightened out, the hourly work force was great about keeping it orderly and clean. Basically, people want to work in an environment that is clean and neat. They have to be shown that it is possible. Also, once the place is straightened out, any new violation stands out and is easy to correct. When the place is a mess, new additions to the mess are lost in the general chaos. Bad housekeeping feeds on itself, but so does good housekeeping.

There are some additional beneficial by-products of having excellent housekeeping. An orderly, clean warehouse is also a safer one. In today's environment of horrendous medical costs and workman's compensation costs, to say nothing about the tragedy of having an employee injured, safety is a key issue. Additionally, you will get favorable reviews from your insurance company and any other agencies doing inspections.

Let's summarize:

- Keep the place neat, clean, and organized.

Information and Data Discipline

An extension of good housekeeping is clean, structured, organized data. In today's world, and particularly in the computer-oriented environment, you cannot survive unless you have accurate, clean data.

The old saying of "garbage in, garbage out" is as valid today as when it was first coined years ago. Modern computer systems have given us stronger tools to deal with this issue, but in the final analysis the entire organization has to believe in the need to keep the data clean and accurate—and make it happen. Again, it is a critical management responsibility.

The best thing that has come along to aid in data accuracy is modern, highly integrated accounting systems. All the elegant edit routines are important, but what has really made the difference is that with all the integration, a single element of data drives a tremendous number of events. Consequently, if an element of data is bad, there are rapid and far-reaching negative consequences. This is desirable, since it creates the feedback that finally forces the necessary discipline required for good data entry.

A problem exists when a system will accept bad data and will process it with no immediate adverse implications. In this situation, the problems emerge much later when it is not clear how the bad data was entered.

I have a wonderful example to illustrate this point. There is a device in our society that requires the operator to input seven or more digits in an exact sequence, with absolutely no errors. Yet this device is operated by our youngest citizens at an extremely early age, and with virtually no difficulty. The device is the telephone.

The reason children learn this task rapidly and accurately is that the system provides immediate reward or punishment in its use. Dial correctly, and you are rewarded by reaching your party. Dial incorrectly, and you get a punitive mechanical sound or someone you don't know.

Contrast this situation to earlier computer systems where a bad stock number could be input, and the only consequence was that a problem would develop long afterwards for someone other than the culprit.

There are two key elements of data that are particularly pertinent in the area of inventory control. The first is sales data; the second is on-hand inventory balances.

Sales information is generally more accurate than on-hand inventory balances. The inherent accuracy of sales data stems from the fact that in modern integrated systems the sales data flows directly from the invoicing function. Stock numbers tend to be correct because the system uses the stock number on the picking slip to cost — and even price — the invoice. Consequently, if the stock number is wrong, a whole array of problems develop that force the correction of the error and prevent the error from repeating.

Ironically, even though sales data tends to be fairly accurate, it is the least sensitive to the penalties of inaccuracy regarding its function in the inventory system. The primary use of sales data is to drive the forecast for each SKU. Accordingly, even if there is some inaccuracy in a single transaction, the worst that happens is a small error is introduced into that particular month of history. The forecasting system itself further minimizes the impact of the error by smoothing that month into the historic past.

On-Hand Balances

The element of data that is of greatest concern is the on-hand balances of each SKU. Almost all modern systems maintain these balances by the "put and take" system (i.e., when product is sold and invoiced, the system "takes," or subtracts, from the balance; when product arrives from the vendor, the system "puts," or adds, to the balance). The "put and take" concept works fine as long as the information is accurate. If a stock number is wrong, however, two errors are created. The SKU that should have been impacted is not updated, and another SKU that should not have been updated is changed.

Additionally, in contrast to the sales data which cleans itself up each month by starting fresh, all inventory balance errors remain in the system perpetuating themselves until they are discovered and corrected.

Modern integrated systems help safeguard against errors by subtracting from the balance via the invoice. Additionally, with an integrated purchase order system, items are added to inventory directly from a release of the purchase order, further minimizing chances for errors.

Despite the safeguards created by integrated systems, there are ways that inventory balances can get fouled up. For example, if the wrong product is pulled from inventory, and the customer does not bring the problem to your attention, then two errors are created. The same is true if the wrong quantity of product is pulled in error.

I do not have any magic solution to the issue of data accuracy. The key is that everyone in the organization must be committed. This means all the classic methods of motivation must be employed. Training, communications, incentives, and above all— leadership on the part of management—are needed to promote data accuracy.

In addition to the "carrot," you have a right to use the "stick." Keeping data entry accurate should be a "condition of employment" in any company today.

Let's summarize:

- If you are not already there, initiate a program to insure that the data you process is as good as humanly possible.

- Demand accuracy. Motivate employees through training, communications, incentives, and management leadership.

- With accurate data in hand, move forward in this book to section two and learn how to simplify and streamline your inventory management system.

Computer-Aided Inventory Management System "Demand Forecasting"

General Discussion

The actions called for in Section One of this book will provide incremental improvements in inventory management, but if you continue to operate by gut feel or subjective decisionmaking, you will deny yourself the quantum improvements possible. To maximize inventory performance, you must take advantage of a computer-oriented inventory management system.

Unfortunately, it is not as simple as grabbing the nearest software package. The history of computerized inventory systems has been less than impressive. Back in the 1970s and early 1980s, most computer systems had inventory management modules that were frankly a joke. You were given basic information about on-hand balances and some sales history that was usually badly displayed. With this meager information, you were supposed to come up with reorder quantities and build a vendor restock order. It was, at best, only slightly better than walking down the aisles with a clipboard.

In the 1980s, computer software started to get more elaborate. The new systems tended to follow one of two conceptional structures. The first systems were designed by theorists and utilized high-powered statistical concepts. Unfortunately, although the techniques were theoretically sound, they were insensitive to the real world of the distributor. The theorists did not take into account the many variables in the ordering process or the numerous constraints placed on distributors by vendors. Much of the data distributors handle does not fit the theoretical pattern and, therefore, does not behave properly. The net result was that these software systems periodically made serious ordering blunders.

The other conceptual approach rejected the statistical methods, either because the designers realized the shortcomings of the methods, or because they just didn't understand the theory in the first place. This group embraced the idea of "simplicity" and developed computer systems based on a series of formalized decisionmaking rules derived from common sense inventory practices and sprinkled with a bit of very basic statistics. These systems were less "dangerous" than the purely theoretical ones, but left a lot to be desired.

Because the "simplicity" systems lack a sound theoretical foundation, they are not powerful in key areas such as forecasting or the determination of the proper safety stock. These systems also tend to be extremely cumbersome to use, requiring extensive manual intervention not only to interject human exception judgement when justified and necessary, but to compensate for their own inherent procedural awkwardness.

The concepts in this book dramatically depart from — and go well beyond — the methods employed by both classical statistics and "simplicity." My concepts, techniques, and computer screens — when incorporated into a computerized inventory management software system — provide the most powerful and reliable inventory replenishment device available. My concepts embrace the rigorous statistical school, but avoid the potential pitfalls. And, in contrast to other systems, my system operates with unbelievable ease and automation, drawing in the human element where the human has some particular knowledge, but not imposing on the human to compensate for weaknesses in the system.

I felt there were tremendous advantages in salvaging the fundamental statistical concepts that had been developed over the decades. These concepts, incidentally, are the foundation of most large, high-powered custom systems used by many mega-retail chains and Fortune 500 corporations. To ignore this body of powerful theory would be like deciding to build a complex bridge, but discarding one hundred years of engineering technology on bridge building with all its sound theory on stresses, tensions, and structure because it's too complicated.

In designing my system, I identified areas where the classic statistical concepts got into trouble and then developed modifications that tempered the problem areas. The resulting system has:

1. A solid theoretical underpinning

2. Easy-to-operate functions requiring limited manual intervention

3. Safeguards that keep the system on track

My software system has been utilized by many distributors. The proof of its effectiveness is that these distributors have realized tremendous success in reducing inventory levels and simultaneously improving order fill rates. Additionally, these distributors now spend a fraction of the time they used to spend on inventory management. It's definitely a win, win, win situation.

I will refer to this system we are going to create as "demand forecasting," since this is the title it has assumed in the various software packages that have incorporated it into their systems.

1.1 Organization of the Following Sections

Each chapter in Section Two is a building block; together, these chapters describe the entire system. Each chapter conveys three aspects of the particular subject under discussion:

- **The concept**
- **The mathematics**
- **The computer application**

It is perfectly okay to skip the sections dealing with mathematics if math is "not your bag" (these areas are shaded in light gray). This information is offered for those who are comfortable with statistics and mathematics, and who wish to understand the inner workings of the system. For others, there is no problem in skipping these areas, since the underlying concepts are thoroughly discussed. Using my system is like driving a high-powered automobile. It's not necessary to know what's going on under the hood to use the device with great effectiveness.

The first two chapters in Section Two deal with the fundamental building blocks of the overall system — the forecast and the reordering logic. Once you understand the forecast and reordering logic, you will begin to see how my system effectively deals with the distributor's unique environment.

Incidentally, as we discuss various concepts, I will allude to "how they operate in your software system," since I am assuming that ultimately each of these concepts will find its way into a computerized system that you will use to manage your inventory. In fact, as I mentioned earlier, there are a number of software systems on the market that incorporate all the concepts we will discuss. These are systems I designed in conjunction with a variety of software houses.

Any inventory control forecasting system will incorporate some form of forward projection of past history. When we consider a system, the real issue is: How effectively does the system process historic data to arrive at a reliable forecast? The accuracy of the forecast is a key factor in determining the effectiveness of the system. A forecast that fails to track trends in demand, or introduces irrelevant spikes or aberrations, will not bring in the right product at the right time.

To achieve a sound, "well-behaved" forecast, we will employ a technique called "exponential smoothing." Additionally, we will introduce a "filter" which screens out wild points (invalid demand history that unduly influences the forecast). Finally, we will introduce a unique technique to seasonally adjust the forecast, thereby recognizing seasonal trends and characteristics of the product.

2.1 Sales Data vs. Demand Data

Before we tackle a discussion about exponential smoothing, let's dispense with the issue of sales data versus demand data. Our forecasting technique can operate effectively with either type of data.

On the surface, it would appear that demand data is the most representative. But, beware! Demand data can sometimes be as misleading as sales data. For example, at Battery and Tire Warehouse we occasionally ran into the situation where Goodyear Rubber Company, whose products we did not carry, would have a production problem on a specific tire. Immediately all the Goodyear stores in the Minneapolis area would run out of that product, and we would suddenly get a tremendous "demand" for the product. If we captured all this "demand," we could have deluded ourselves that future sales would be significant and stock up accordingly. Once Goodyear's problem passed, however, we no longer were the supplier of choice.

On other occasions, we would get six "demands" for a given type of unusual tire. In reality, all six demands were actually only one demand coming through six different jobbers who were shopping around for the item for one actual customer. Sales data also has its problems, particularly when you miss sales as a result of being out of stock. Nevertheless, sales data at least has the advantage of being based on bona fide transactions; it also is easier to capture. Under our system, the out-of-stock problem will be less of an issue because we will more consistently have the items in the right place at the right time. Moreover, built-in safeguards will alert us to months that are significantly depressed due to chronic stock-out problems.

For these reasons, and because capturing demand data creates an added burden on the system, I recommend that we use sales data to build our forecast.

To begin, let's review the concept of simple averaging as a foundation for the discussion of exponential averaging. In a simple five-month moving average, the most recent five months of history are added together and then divided by five. The result is a straight, unweighted average of the five months. Every month, a new month of demand is added, and the oldest month is dropped.

The net effect of simple averaging is that each month carries the same weight in the calculation until it is six months old, and then it is dropped out completely. This is not a particularly bad system, and it is the basis for many inventory software packages being offered, but its simplicity is its flaw. In the sales and distribution business, it is unreasonable that information should have the exact same weighing for five months, and then drop to zero, as if the sixth month suddenly had no relevance. This is not just an academic issue since this characteristic can have specific adverse impact on the forecast.

Here is an example of how the simple moving average can break down:

> Let's say your last forecast was for 100 units per month. The new month comes in at 120 units. You then update the forecast by averaging in the new data. Using simple averaging and working with five months of data, it is possible for the new forecast to come in *lower than the old forecast* if the month that you dropped had been overwhelming the average.

Consider the following example:

Month	JAN	FEB	MAR	APR	MAY	JUNE	JULY	AUG
Sales	89	92	135	98	87	89	91	120

- Forecast for August is 100 (March through July divided by 5)
- Forecast for September is 97 (April through August divided by 5)

Note that the new forecast goes in the wrong direction! The premise of a forecast is that it is "learning" from the new data. Simple averaging, however, can cause the forecast to "learn" incorrectly.

In contrast to the simple moving average, an exponential average *will always move in the direction of the new data,* and is, in fact, a superior method of forecasting future demand.

An exponential average (or forecast) is similar in concept to a moving average, but with some very significant differences. In an exponential average, each month is weighted at an ever-declining amount, so that as the data becomes older, its influence on the average (or forecast) is less and less. The nature of the weight of each month is determined by an "exponential decay curve."

Exhibit A is an example of an exponential decay curve. The shape of the decay curve is set by a multiplier called an "alpha level." The alpha level is an arbitrary number selected for the effect it has on the data. A high alpha level will cause the forecast to respond quickly to new data and fade out the influence of old data. A low alpha level will cause the forecast to respond more slowly to new data and to retain the influence of old data. The curve in this example is based on an alpha level of .30. Over the years, I have had experience with a tremendous variety of product types, and I have discovered that an alpha level of .30 is a nice balance between the extremes. (We will discuss the alpha level in greater detail in Section 2.2.2.)

Exhibit A

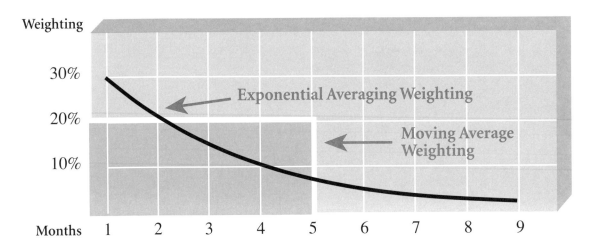

Note: On this curve, the most current month is weighted at .30, the second at .21, and the third at .15. Each weighing reflects the effect of using an alpha level of .30.

Another way of looking at exponential averaging is as follows: A new month of sales history is introduced with a weight of .30. Next month this item of data moves down the line and has its weighing dropped to .21; the next month it drops to .15; and so on until it simply phases out of having an influence on the forecast.

The method by which all this complex weighing occurs is surprisingly simple. The formula for updating an exponential average is as follows:

New Average = Old Average x (1.0 - Alpha) + New Month History x Alpha

To use some actual numbers:
Last Month's Average (or Forecast)   **= 120 Units**
New Month's Actual Sales   **= 140 Units**

New Average = 120 x (1.0-.30) + 140 x .30
$$= 84 + 42$$
$$= 126$$

By successively applying this formula each month, you will create an exponential average that exhibits the effects of weighing. Incidentally, the weight applied to data never drops completely to zero, and even after many months, the system is still giving at least some trivial weight to the month in question. The key point, however, is that in contrast to the moving average, the data doesn't drop off suddenly but rather just fades out of the system.

Again, because of its characteristics, an exponential average will always move in the direction of the new data — in contrast to a moving average, which will not.

The reason for dwelling on this difference between the two systems of forecasting is that some other inventory management systems actually use a moving average as their forecasting technique.

Over a vast array of applications, an exponential average will do an excellent job of tracking trends and patterns for just about all commercial-type sales data, and will give a good indication of future sales for that item.

Now that we have covered the basic concepts of the forecast, it is necessary to introduce some of the issues that arise when we begin to make use of the technique.

Initializing the Average

The exponential average is calculated by successive applications of the formula just outlined. In the real world, we have to deal with one very practical issue that relates to "the starting point." If we were to run these calculations starting with an initial average of zero, the forecast would be constantly understated because of the influence of this first data point of zero. Conversely, if we were to use the first item of data as our starting average, it would exert an undue amount of influence until it was phased out with the passage of time.

A very simple technique will compensate for this problem. Take all the months of data you have for a specific SKU (but I wouldn't bother using more than a year's worth), and calculate a simple arithmetic average. Set that "average" as the starting point. This technique very effectively stabilizes the system, and then allows the future calculations to refine and update the forecast.

This "initial averaging" approach performs one additional function. When an item is relatively new, and there are only two or three months of data, it is "rolling" in some extra weighting to the few months in question, thereby making it unnecessary to consider some form of graduated alpha level for new products. The table below shows what the weighting would be if we had only three months of data, and then what it would be if we had four months of data, and five.

Weighting Based on Months of Data

Month	Three	Four	Five
February			.14
March		.19	.15
April	.28	.22	.18
May	.33	.26	.22
June	.39	.33	.31

Let's define more clearly what this table is illustrating. The first column of figures is the weighting that results from our initialization technique when we have only three months of data (the first month being April). June is weighted at .39, May at .33, and April at .28. When we base our calculations on four months of data (starting in March), we arrive at the figures in the second column. When we use five months of of data (starting with February), we arrive at the figures in the third column. Note how the weighting factors approach the classical figures of .30, .21, and .15. as the number of months of data increases.

Incidentally, this technique of initializing the average is one of many modifications we will make so that the theoretical statistics work in the real world environment.

2.2.2 **The Alpha Level**

The alpha level sets the shape of the decay curve or, in other words, the rate of decay of the weighing of the data. The higher the alpha level, the more the average will respond to new data and fade out the influence of the old data. The lower the alpha level, the slower it will respond to new data; but it will give greater importance to the old data. There is, again, an analogy to a moving average. As more months are included in the moving average, the average will be more stable, but less responsive to new information. The converse is true if fewer months are used.

As I stated earlier, from years of experience I have found that an alpha level of .30 is a good compromise. If you feel that your product line is in a state of extremely rapid change, and you would like to use a higher alpha level such as .40, or even .50, you can do so. Keep in mind, however, that this action involves other considerations. Using the higher level will cause the system to respond very quickly not only to new data, but to random movements as well.

Conversely, if your product line is relatively stable, you might opt to use a lower alpha level such as .20, or even .10. This level will cause the forecast to be steadier, but it will also cause it to be sluggish in responding to new trends and patterns of demand.

Having covered the mechanics of the exponential average, I want to point out some of the pitfalls of the concept (and for that matter, any forecasting system) and the safeguards I have developed to compensate for these situations.

On occasion, any sales data can contain some spikes in demand that would be misleading if used to update the forecast. A classic example would be a one-time export order, or an order from a manufacturer who makes a one-time buy of substantial quantities.

The exponential averaging system will tend to "smooth out" these spikes in demand, but if the figure is sufficiently out of line, it will nevertheless distort the new forecast. To cope with this problem, I want to introduce a filtering concept whose function will be to spot these spikes, screen the data down to a more logical level, and further smooth the new forecast.

The Filter System – How It's Created

Before we can create our filtering system, we must introduce another concept called the Mean Average Deviation or MAD. The MAD is simply an exponential average of the errors (ignoring whether the errors were plus or minus) between the forecast and the actual data. (If the forecast was for 125 units to be sold in March, and 137 were actually sold, then the error was 12 units. This error is then smoothed into the average of the past errors and presented as the MAD.) The calculations for updating the MAD by exponential averaging are the same as discussed earlier, except that we are using the errors rather than the actual sales data.

Example:

Month	Actual Sales	Exp. Ave.	FCST.	Error	M.A.D.
Jun	34	30.0	29.0	5.0	5.3
Feb	37	32.1	30.0	7.0	5.8
Mar	35	33.0	32.1	2.9	4.9
Apr	42	35.7	33.0	9.0	6.1
May	36	35.8	35.7	.3	4.4
June	38	36.5	35.8	2.2	3.7

The above table illustrates the calculations for both an exponential average and for the MAD. Going across the columns using April, we have actual sales of 42. The new exponential average is 35.7 (the last average of 33 times .7, plus the 42 times .3). The forecast for April was the exponential average of 33 from March. The error then is 9 (the difference of the actual 42 less the forecast of 33). The MAD is then 6.1 (the past MAD of 4.9 times .7 plus the new error of 9 times .3).

Here we have the same problem we encountered earlier relative to starting out or initializing the average error. The initialization process can be achieved by the same technique we used earlier, namely taking a simple arithmetic average of the errors for which we have data, and setting that as the first item of data.

The MAD is a measurement of the normal variation of the data for that SKU. Consequently, we can employ this measurement to create our filter. We can state from classical statistics that three times the MAD added to the average will establish an outer band, outside of which only three percent of the new sales points will fall due to normal random variation. Four times the MAD is even further out, and only one percent of the points are expected to fall outside this range.

With this insight, we are going to set a band at four MADs and then say that any new sales data in excess of this level is highly suspicious and most likely does not represent our normal sales history.

The filter operates by checking the sales level of each new month against the band of variation of that SKU; if the data falls outside the band, it is adjusted down to the upper range of that band. The band width, as we stated, is four MADs above the average.

For example, if the average is 120 units and the MAD is 15 units, then four MADs is 60 — added to 120 is 180. If the new month of history comes in at 410, the system will recognize that this is totally out of line with history, and will knock the figure down to 180. The filtered figure of 180 will then be exponentially averaged to create the new forecast.

Later on, we will talk about an approach whereby this filtering action is highlighted during the reordering process. Then, if you are aware of the details behind the spike in the data, you will be able to alter the history down to its proper level. The system will then use your new adjusted data in the future — with no need to filter.

A key point is that the filter operates *automatically* and will protect the system against wild points even if the operator fails to intervene. Just about all other systems *require* manual intervention. In our case, we will invite manual intervention if the operator has some contribution to make, but we will be "fail safe" in either regard.

It is possible to use a band width of greater or fewer MADs, but I would advise extreme caution. Again, there are consequences to any action. For example, if you narrow the band by using only three MADs, the system will more readily kick out points; conversely, it will also be less sensitive to bona fide new trends represented by this higher new level of demand.

The MAD, incidentally, is a critical figure that we will use later when we discuss the reorder target calculation. The MAD tells us the reliability of each forecast for each specific SKU, and thereby influences the amount of safety stock that is maintained.

2.2.6 Introducing Seasonality

An exponential average will do an excellent job of tracking trends and patterns, and will provide a good forecast of upcoming demand. If, however, the data has a distinct seasonal pattern, the standard exponential average will start to have problems.

It will tend to lag behind the patterns of seasonal strengthening and weakening. More seriously, it will miss the turning points when the season either peaks or hits bottom. At these times, it will over- or under-forecast, bringing in product at the wrong time or failing to bring in product when it is badly needed.

Incidentally, seasonality can exist in sales data for reasons other than weather. There may be a distinct pattern due to factors such as the school year, tax season, or holidays.

2.2.6.1 Seasonality – Some Problems in Application

Classical statistics offer an elegant system for introducing seasonality to the exponential smoothing technique. The problem, however, is that the technique falls apart when applied in its original concept to typical sales history that is encountered in the real world. Extreme errors are introduced into the forecast if the data is anything but strong in volume, free of wild points, and supported by two full years of history. By this definition, we have just rejected 80 percent of the data with which we typically deal.

Our objective, therefore, is to retain and take advantage of the simple and clean computational features of the classical statistical concept, but compensate for the problems created by the data typically encountered in the distribution industry.

The classical statistical technique internally develops the seasonality pattern for each SKU with the data of that SKU. This is where it gets into trouble, since *each* SKU is subject to all the problems mentioned earlier. The key to solving the problem of seasonality is this: to conclude that each SKU does not have its own unique seasonality pattern, but does belong to a family of products that move to an overall pattern of seasonality.

For example, a battery for a 1986 Toronado does not have a distinctly different seasonal pattern of demand than, let's say, battery for a 1989 Escort. The batteries from these cars will have different levels of demand, but the relationship of sales in June versus January will be similar.

Accordingly, we will attack the issue of seasonality as follows:

1. The user must first determine the families of products that have a similar set of seasonal characteristics. Note: Many products will *not* have a seasonal pattern, and these can be classified accordingly.

2. Having established each family, we then select three or four specific SKUs that are going to act as the representatives of this entire family. The SKUs that we choose will be ones which have a strong level of demand, and for which we have two or three full years of data. Since we are going to use only four SKUs, we can gather the data manually if necessary.

The method of calculating the seasonality indices for a given set of data is as follows:

1. Use only full years of data. The data can start at any month, but you cannot use less than twelve months.

2. Organize the data on a spread sheet in the format shown below:

Example:

	Mar	Apr	May	June	July	Aug	Sept	Oct	Nov	Dec	Jan	Feb
1993	12	14	21	24	19	27	45	65	71	45	22	9
1992	9	7	12	18	21	22	35	56	59	39	14	5
1991	10	11	13	24	18	25	41	44	52	32	65	6

(The example above is for one SKU—you would have another one, two, or three additionally.)

3. Scan the data to insure that the seasonal pattern you thought should be there is truly there and reasonably consistent between items (the example above would certainly imply a valid seasonal pattern).

4. Look for spikes in the data that appear to have nothing to do with seasonality and may be aberrations due to one-time buys. Manually modify this data with values that make more sense, considering the values in adjacent months. (January of 1991, with a value of 65, looks completely out of line, and should be arbitrarily adjusted to a value of, let's say, 13.)

5. Add all the same month's values together to get the total SKUs for that month. Next, add the totals from all the months to get a grand total. Then divide each month's total by the grand total and multiply by 12.

Prior Example Continued:

	Mar	Apr	May	June	July	Aug	Sept	Oct	Nov	Dec	Jan	Feb
Total	31	32	46	66	58	74	121	165	182	116	49*	20
	(* 13 was used vs. the 65 in 1991)					(Grand Total: 960)						
Index No.	.4	.4	.6	.8	.7	.9	1.5	2.0	2.3	1.5	.6	.3

6. Round the resulting figures to the nearest one decimal, but be sure the total of all twelve numbers equals 12.0 (October was dropped by .1 to 2.0 to get the total to 12).

7. Modify the index numbers you have created to "clean up" any dips or peaks that do not make sense (e.g., in the above example, one could question if the June through August figures make sense or whether they should be "smoothed" to .7, .8, and .9, indicating a gradual rise during that part of the season).

The commercial software systems developed to my concepts perform the above manipulations in a separate "off-line" routine.

There is one other alternative to the process. It is also possible to use total sales data for a group of products that fall into a single family. This data can be either in units or dollars. Be careful, however, to insure that the total history is truly for a single family of products that have the same seasonality. This data can then be processed in the exact same fashion as discussed above.

Once the seasonal index is established for the family of products, we then "tag" each product in the family with a code that will let the system know to pull its associated seasonality indices for the full calculation that will be described shortly.

A seasonal index is something you create initially, and then update every few years if there is reason to suspect that the indices may have become outdated. Every few years may seem too infrequent, but keep in mind that we are dealing with a fairly stable phenomenon. Products rarely shift their patterns relative to seasons, if at all.

The set of seasonal indices we have created will be used to calculate the "seasonally adjusted exponential average." There are many advantages to this concept of using "families" of products for seasonal adjustment:

a. We now have a series, developed from good solid data, that can act as the seasonality guide for the weaker, more unstable items.

b. The index has been cleansed of wild points that have nothing to do with seasonality.

c. The indices can be used for a new SKU of the same family, even if only a few months of real data are available.

2.2.6.3 Seasonality – The Actual Calculations

To arrive at a seasonally adjusted exponential average, we first calculate a "Deseasonalized Exponential Average," and then update it with "Deseasonalized Monthly Demand."

Deseasonalizing is accomplished by dividing the new monthly demand by the seasonal index for that month. For example, if we sold 120 units in a month, and the seasonal index for that month was 1.2, then by dividing the 1.2 into the 120 we get a deseasonalized demand of 100. The formula is as follows:

New DEA = Old DEA x (1.0 - Alpha)
+ (New Monthly Demand/Seasonal Index) x Alpha

Using actual numbers:
      Old DEA = 100
      New Monthly demand = 144
      Seasonal Index for that Month = 1.2
New DEA = 100 x .70 + (144/1.2) x .3
= 70 + 36
= 106

Note: In our example, the seasonally adjusted demand for the month came in stronger than expected, and therefore the deseasonalized average was increased from 100 to 106.

Okay. This tells us how to calculate the DEA, but what is the forecast? The forecast is simply the latest calculated DEA times the seasonality index for the month in question. In our example above, if the following month had an index of .90 (demand seasonally starts to plunge), then the forecast for that month would be 95 (106 x .9 and then rounded).

Seasonality – Critical Characteristics

My forecasting system has two critical features that make it superior to other forecasting systems:

a. In the new forecast, seasonality is comprehended automatically and effectively, without requiring manual involvement. Manual intervention is always possible, however, if desired by the end user.

b. The deseasonalized average will trend up or down to reflect strengthening or weakening of demand *even during the off-season.* In other words, if an item is becoming more popular during the off-season, the system will nevertheless note this trend, and strengthen the deseasonalized average. Then when the strong part of the season hits, the system will spring off the higher base average to forecast a higher demand than actually occurred during the same time as the prior year.

   The same will be true if the item is loosing popularity. The deseasonalized average will be dropping - even during the strong part of the season — and then as the slow season arrives, the forecast will multiply the new lower deseasonalized average by the depressed index number. The net result would be to bring in less stock for this item which is dropping in demand.

These are major advantages, since just about any other system utilizes the actual demand of the prior year, which is by definition a full year old.

2.3   An Example of the System in Actual Use

Exhibit B is a printout of a screen from a specific software package that utilizes this method of forecasting. In this system, this information for a particular SKU can be called up, and it will display a "simulation" of the forecast for that SKU, starting with the first month of data through the most current month. It is not something you would normally bother with, but is available for special situations where you might want to see how the system arrived at its forecast.

At this point, the screen is ideal for demonstrating the calculations we have been discussing, starting with an item that has *no* seasonality.

Exhibit B

Calculations for Item: 412302   Location: Minnesota

Month		Hist. SLS	Filter	SEAS	D.E.A.	M.A.D.	Frcst.	Error
Jan	1991	18	N/A	1.0	32.6	20.8	38.8	20.8
Feb	1991	25	N/A	1.0	30.3	8.9	32.6	7.6
Mar	1991	25	N/A	1.0	28.7	6.0	30.3	5.3
Apr	1991	12	N/A	1.0	23.7	13.5	28.7	16.7
May	1991	32	N/A	1.0	26.2	10.4	23.7	8.3-
Jun	1991	30	0	1.0	27.3	7.1	26.2	3.8-
Jul	1991	30	0	1.0	28.1	5.3	27.3	2.7-
Aug	1991	86	49	1.0	34.4	10.0	28.1	57.9-
Sep	1991	37	0	1.0	35.2	7.8	34.4	2.6-
Oct	1991	62	0	1.0	43.2	13.5	35.2	26.8-
Nov	1991	57	0	1.0	47.3	13.6	43.2	13.8-
Dec	1991	52	0	1.0	48.7	10.9	47.3	4.7-
Jan	(MTD)	7		1.0				

This exhibit is for a "specific truck tire" belonging to a "family of tires" that does not have a discernible seasonal characteristic. (Note that column 4, headed "SEAS" is all 1.0s.)

A discussion of the other columns is as follows:

MONTH Self explanatory

HIST SLS The actual sales history

FILTER   This is the filtering system that was discussed in detail earlier. The N/A shown in the first five months simply means that the system has made no attempt at filtering any data, since it has no basis for filtering until some history is established. Note that in August, the demand of 86 units was out of line with past history, and the system dropped the demand to 49. One could argue that 86 was not excessively out of line, but the key point is that if the number had been 586, the system would also have dropped it to 49.

SEAS Seasonality Index for the family of products of which the specific SKU is a member. (These are all 1.0 since we are dealing with a product that has no seasonality.)

DEA This is the Deseasonalized Exponential Average, and since in this example there is no seasonality, it is the same as a regular exponential average. You can trace the calculations based on the formulas offered earlier. For example, December's DEA of 48.7 was arrived at by taking 47.3 x (1.0 -.3) + 52 x .30.

MAD This is the Mean Average Deviation. It was calculated by exponentially averaging the errors (far right column) without regard to the plus or minus sign. For example, the 13.5 MAD for October was arrived at by taking 7.8 (September MAD) x (1.0 - .3) + 26.8 (October Error) x .30.

FORECAST This is the actual forecast the system uses, and because our SKU has no seasonality, it is nothing more than the exponential average of the prior month. For example, the November forecast of 43.2 was the DEA from October.

ERROR This is the error of the forecast (the sales history column minus the forecast).

Exhibit C is the same as Exhibit B except that we are now looking at a heavy duty battery that has a seasonality pattern. The columns are the same as discussed earlier.

Exhibit C

Calculations for Item: 8DG1150   Location: 1

Month		Hist. SLS	Filter	SEAS	D.E.A.	M.A.D.	Frcst.	Error
Jan	1991	200	N/A	1.1	153.3	44.8	155.2	44.8-
Feb	1991	85	N/A	1.0	132.8	66.0	153.3	68.3
Mar	1991	172	N/A	0.8	157.5	65.8	106.2	65.8-
Apr	1991	103	N/A	0.8	148.9	35.8	126.0	23.0
May	1991	113	N/A	0.9	141.9	26.9	134.0	21.0
Jun	1991	98	0	0.8	136.1	21.2	113.5	15.5
Jul	1991	102	0	0.8	133.5	15.5	108.9	6.9
Aug	1991	162	0	1.0	142.1	19.4	133.5	28.5-
Sep	1991	180	0	1.2	144.5	16.4	170.5	9.5-
Oct	1991	150	0	1.3	135.8	22.9	187.9	37.9
Nov	1991	170	0	1.3	134.3	18.0	176.5	6.5
Dec	1991	158	0	1.1	137.1	15.0	147.7	10.3-
Jan	(MTD)	14		1.1				

Note that the seasonality column in this example has a distinct set of indices that describe a product that has relatively low demand during the spring and summer, then starts to gain in popularity, with peak demand occurring in October and November.

This set of indices resides in the system for a family of products all having this pattern. The battery — 8DG1150 — has been tagged as belonging to this family and the indices noted were pulled accordingly.

There are two key differences between this example in Exhibit C and the earlier one in Exhibit B.

a. In updating the DEA, the actual history was deseasonalized by dividing it by the seasonal index for that month. For example, December DEA of 137.1 was arrived at by applying the formula that we developed in section 2.2.6.3: 134.3 x (1.0 - .3) + (158/1.1) x .3 = 137.1.

b. The forecast is the DEA for the prior month, multiplied by the seasonal index for the month being forecasted. For example, the December forecast of 147.7 is November's DEA of 134.3 times December's index of 1.1.

A Special Situation – Very Strong Seasonality

A special situation exists when the product group or family has very strong seasonality, and just about all the demand occurs in three to four months. This is true of products such as suntan lotion, air conditioning parts, and snow tires.

The theoretical statistical techniques for handling seasonally adjusted exponential averaging break down when the data contains radical seasonality.

There is a way, however, to modify the classical approach so that we keep the power of the concept while circumventing the problems to which I have been alluding.

Why There Is a Problem

Keep in mind that every time we update the forecast, it is "learning" from the new data. Under normal conditions this works fine and the forecast is constantly adjusting to the new input, picking up new trends and patterns.

If we have radical seasonality, then some of the months will have seasonal index numbers that are extremely small (e.g., .1 or .2).

Let's assume that the deseasonalized average for a given item is running at 100 units, and the index for the next month is .1. The forecast for the next month is then 10 units (100 times .1). Now let's assume that we happen to sell 20 units. — No big deal! — Ten extra units could have been sold for a variety of random reasons.

When the system updates the deseasonalized average, it notes that actual sales were 200 percent of the forecast, and proceeds to boost the deseasonalized average unreasonably (from 100 to 130). Then, when we get to the strong season with an index of 2.5, the system takes this artificially boosted deseasonalized average, multiplies it by the 2.5 index, and arrives at a forecast that is way too high.

The solution to this problem is to recognize that we really do not want the forecast to "learn" during the periods of very low seasonal demand. Random fluctuations can have too strong an effect on the forecast and can lead to very bad inventory decisions. To solve this problem, we need to use the system as described earlier, except that during periods when the seasonal index is below a level of roughly .4, we must let the system "mark time" and not be updated. In other words, we must hold the deseasonalized average at its current level whenever the most recent month to be updated has a seasonal index at or below our cutoff point.

In this situation, it is necessary to process more than one year of data. Normally, one year of data is sufficient, since weighing the data once it is beyond eight months becomes virtually trivial. If we are updating the average with only three or four months of the year, then we need more years of data to establish a meaningful figure.

The Reorder Target – General Discussion 3.0

At the heart of the demand forecasting system is the "reorder target." It drives the actual quantities that will be ordered at the time of building an order on a specific vendor. At the time of ordering, it is the figure that is compared to the amount of product both on hand and in the pipeline, and the difference is what is recommended to be ordered.

For example, if the reorder target is 135 and the on-hand balance less any committed product is 30, and there are 45 units on order, then the system will recommend a new order of 60. (The 30 on hand, plus the 45 on order equals 75, which is 60 less than the reorder target of 135.)

Note that we use a single number for the reorder target, instead of a "min-max," or "order/line point." These other concepts are an outgrowth of earlier work in the inventory control field, and are less effective.

The Reorder Target – Its Components 3.1

The reorder target is comprised of two components.

The first is called "Basic Coverage" or BC. This refers to providing adequate product to cover the forecasted rate at which the product will be consumed during the period between reorders, plus the lead time for the product to actually arrive. The formula for BC is as follows:

BC = Forecast x (LT/4 + OF/4)

> **The forecast was developed in section 2.0**
> **LT is the lead time in weeks for the product to arrive**
> **OF is the reorder frequency in weeks**

The second component of the reorder target is the "Safety Stock" or SS, which is the quantity of product that the system deems should be on hand to compensate for the inevitable inaccuracy of the forecast. Consequently, this calculation will utilize the MAD, which is a measurement of the error levels of the forecast for each particular SKU.

The formula to calculate the Safety Stock (SS) is as follows:

SS = SF x MAD x [.1 + .07 (LT+ OF)]

SF is the safety factor that determines the desired order fill performance. This safety factor comes from the following table:

Order Fill	Desired Safety Factor
98%	2.6
97%	2.4
95%	2.0
90%	1.6
85%	1.3
80%	1.1

(You can interpolate the values given above if an order fill level falls between the ones listed.)

The full formula for calculating the Reorder Target (RT) is as follows:

RT = Basic Coverage (BC) + Safety Stock (SS)

or:

RT = Forecast x (LT/4 + OF/4) + SF x MAD x [.1 + .07 (LT+ OF)]
Using actual numbers:
LT = 2 weeks
OF = 4 weeks
Forecast = 60 units/month
MAD = 27

Percent Fill Desired = 95% (which will call for a 2.0 SF from the table)

Then:

RT = 60 x (2/4 + 4/4) + (2.0 x 27) x [.1 + .07 (2 + 4)]
RT = 60 x (6/4) + 54 x (.1 +.42)
RT = 90 + (54 x .52)
RT = 90 + 28
RT = 118

In the above example, the system is stating that it needs 90 units, either on hand or in the pipeline, to cover the anticipated demand during the period between when that product is going to arrive and the next opportunity to reorder. It also needs 28 units (for a total of 118) to cover for the inaccuracy of the forecast, so that over a period of time we can expect a statistical average order fill of 95 percent.

Special Features of Our Safety Stock Calculation

One school of thought supports using a "straight percent" of the forecast as the safety stock. The rationale is, "This is an adequate approach — why get complicated?" It is adequate when compared to "eyeballing" data or ordering off a clipboard while walking down the aisles, but it is mediocre when compared to the safety stock system we will employ.

The entire function of the safety stock is to compensate for the inaccuracy of the forecast. Consequently, to ignore the MAD, which measures the accuracy of the forecast, is to ignore a key measurement.

To appreciate the implications of the two systems, consider the following scenario. When a product is newly introduced, it has a relatively low demand level since there is a small customer base using the product. Moreover the accuracy of the forecast is poor because the small customer base introduces erratic demands. During this period the "champions of simplicity" would lay in a safety stock of some fixed percent of the demand. This safety level would be too low, however, and lead to stock outages at the very time you are trying to establish the product.

By recognizing the MAD, we would appreciate the erratic demand and put in safety stocks to compensate for the problem, thereby giving the fill levels desired.

As the product matures and the customer base expands, the demand levels increase substantially, and the item becomes significantly more predictable due to the normal compensating errors inherent in a popular item.

Again, our "champions of simplicity" would now lay in a safety stock based on a fixed percent of the forecast. This would be well in excess of what is needed. Our system, however, will back off on the safety stock and thereby improve our inventory utilization. Multiply this scenario a few hundred times and you are talking about a significant difference in inventory performance.

Simulating the Reorder Process

How the system operates can best be understood by tracking a simulation of the system in action. This simulation can be achieved by graphing over a period of time the level of inventories, as if they were being driven by the reorder target calculation. We will use the figures developed in Section 3.1 for our example.

We will impose one key simplification on our example to make it more understandable. The forecast and Mean Average Deviation (MAD) will be kept constant throughout, when, in fact, in a "live situation" the system would be updating both with new data to stay current with the evolving pattern of demand.

Let's trace the logic of this process in the exhibit below, starting in week one.

Exhibit D

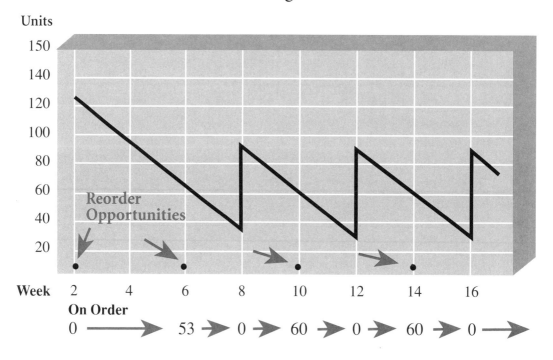

Reorder Target Simulation

Remember, we are using the figures from our earlier example in Section 3.1, where the forecast of monthly demand was 60 units per month, the MAD was 27, etc.

Note: In Exhibit D, week zero, we set the inventory at 155 units (deliberately high) to illustrate how the system will clean up this imbalance and settle down to a logical level. The inventory drops steadily at the rate of 60 units per month. At week two, we have our first opportunity to reorder. Since the amount on hand (125), plus on order (0), is more than the reorder target of 118, we do not reorder.

The inventory continues to drop at the rate of 60 units per month. At week six, we again have an opportunity to reorder. This time the amount on hand is 65, which is less than the RT of 118, and we order 53 (118 less the 65 on hand). The inventory continues to drop, but in week eight the order placed two weeks earlier arrives, bringing the inventory up to 88.

The inventory starts dropping again at the rate of 60 units per month, and in week ten we can reorder. The amount on hand is 58, so we order 60. In week twelve the 60 arrive, bringing our inventory back up to 88. By now the system has settled down to a routine, and will repeat the "saw tooth" pattern indefinitely. Again, keep in mind that in actual practice the forecast would not be perfect, and the system would look different, but the concept is the same.

Let's look at the simulation in Exhibit E to gain additional insight into the process. In this case we will use the same forecast and MAD as before, but we will switch the lead time to four weeks and the order frequency to two weeks (the exact reverse of our previous example). The "basic coverage" would still be 90 units and the "safety stock" would stay at 28 units (since the total of LT + SF is still 6 weeks). The reorder target would therefore still be at 118. Exhibit E is the simulation of this new set of conditions.

Reorder Target Simulation

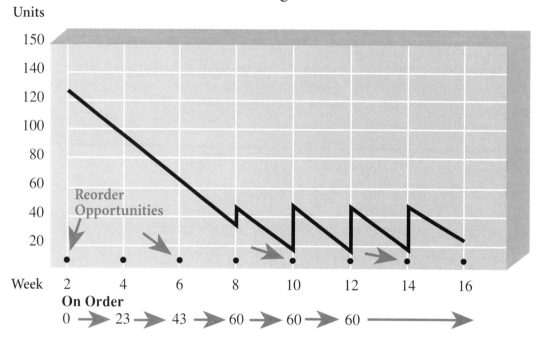

Note that the process in Exhibit E is similar to the process in Exhibit D. The first time product is put on order is in week four, when 23 units are ordered to reach the reorder target of 118. In week six, another 30 units are ordered; and in week eight, another 30. The 23 ordered in week four arrive, however, increasing the inventory and dropping the amount on order. By week eight, the saw tooth pattern that repeats itself indefinitely is established.

The two graphs illustrate a key concept. The ability to order frequently is more important than lead time in keeping inventory down and order fill up. The average amount of inventory in our first example is 58 units; the average in the second is 33.

Note: In the second example, most of the product is in the "pipeline" and not in stock. This is ideal, since product doesn't start to incur carrying costs until it arrives at the warehouse.

So far, we have assumed that the forecast was perfect each month. Now let's assume that the forecast in our first example is in error starting in week eight. In the graph below, we have reproduced our original example, but superimposed a new rate with inventory starting to decline in week eight, corresponding to a sales rate of 90 units (in contrast to the forecast of 60). This is the gray line.

Exhibit F

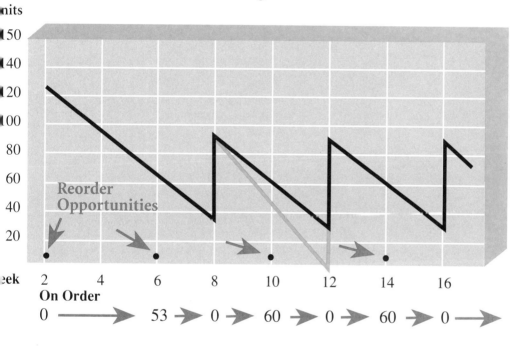

Reorder Target Simulation

In this example, we will be out of stock for only a few days until the replenishment order arrives. The safety stock did its job of providing product to cover for the higher-than-forecasted sales rate in that month.

Keep in mind that in actual use, the system would update the forecast and the MAD, and increase both the MAD and the forecast for the future.

4.0 Critical Parameters – Lead Time, Reorder Frequency and Safety Factor

Having discussed the theory behind two key elements of the system — the forecast and the reorder target — we are ready to start thinking about the actual reordering process. Before we get to it, however, we need to more thoroughly develop three concepts which were introduced earlier.

These concepts — lead time, reorder frequency, and safety factor — tend to be unique to each particular vendor or product category. Two of them are subject to change throughout the year, but all three deserve particular attention and discussion at this point.

4.1 Safety Factor

The safety factor drives the reorder target, and particularly the safety stock part of the reorder target, to achieve a desired level of order fill (see Section 3.1). Generally, but not necessarily, the level will be the same across all vendor groups, and will stay the same throughout the year. (It would be unusual, but not impossible, to desire different service levels at different times of the year and between product groups.)

There is a school of thought that proposes an ABC-type concept, which sets safety stock at different levels for different classes of product to give different fill rates. The theory is based on the idea that some products are very critical (e.g., have higher gross profit margins) and we are willing to have more safety stock to achieve very high levels of service, while other products are less critical and we can skimp on their stock.

My demand forecasting system will certainly accommodate these ideas. I question the basic theory, however. I know that in my business, my customers expect a certain fill level for all the products I have gone one record as stocking (authorized stock list), and could care less about my relative profit margins. A great benefit of my demand forecasting system is that inventory performance improves so dramatically that it is unnecessary to use techniques such as the ABC concepts.

In the formulas discussed earlier in Section 3.1, the safety factor was expressed in terms of a percent (such as 95 percent). The inference is that if you set the parameter to the 95 percent level, you will enjoy a 95 percent order fill. While this conclusion is somewhat valid, reality is a bit more complex.

Safety stock is intended to compensate for the inaccuracy of the forecast. It is a very theoretical concept, however, and the statistician's idea of order fill is different from the distributor's. The statistician's definition of 95 percent performance is that there is only a five percent chance that the item will be out of stock during a replenishment cycle. The entire period during which the product first arrives and the inventory is at its maximum is ignored. At this time, we are giving 100 percent fill on the product. Consequently, the statistician is vastly understating the service levels that occur on a day-to-day basis.

On the other side of the coin, the theoretical concept does not take into account the unreliability of the supplying vendor. In other words, if the vendor fails to ship a particular SKU, there is no provision in the safety stock to compensate for this failure. Note however, that the safety stock will provide some protection for this situation since it is quite possible that at the time of the vendor back-order there is no excess demand for the product. The safety stock ends up compensating for the vendor's back-order after all.

Keep in mind that it is not possible to adequately compensate for a vendor's back-order by increasing the safety stock. When a vendor fails to ship a specific SKU, he will usually not ship any of the desired item. Therefore, the safety stock would have to be gigantic to offset this failure. Additionally, since you have no way of knowing which items will be back-ordered, adding safety stock across the board would require prohibitive amounts of inventory.

I recommend that you start with the percent figure that corresponds to the order fill desired, but then adjust the number up or down over a few months until the system is responding at levels that feel comfortable.

A word of caution: As you seek order fill levels above 90 percent, the amount of safety stock increases significantly; over 97 percent, the safety stock starts becoming prohibitive. For most businesses, 95 percent is a reasonable compromise.

4.2   Reorder Frequency

Reorder frequency is one of the more confusing issues, and yet one of the most important. Flatly stated, reducing the time interval between reorders is the single most important variable in improving inventory turns while simultaneously increasing order fill.

Generally, two factors determine the reorder frequency. They are lead time and vendor constraints.

4.2.1   Reorder Frequency – Vendor Constrained

Reorder frequency is generally determined by the pricing policy of the vendor as it relates to each specific shipment. The vendor typically establishes a price structure annually for each distributor, based on the total buying potential of the distributor. The cost of each order, however, is influenced by the size of that particular order. Unless a full truckload is ordered, freight is not prepaid; unless the order hits an arbitrary dollar or unit amount, there is a premium over the base price. In the latter case, the vendor has established a pricing break point to force his customers into order quantities that he can efficiently handle.

In both situations, the time interval between reordering becomes the length of time required to generate sufficient product requirements to hit the shipping minimum or full truckload. For example, if your monthly sales of a particular vendor's product add up to about 80,000 pounds, and a full truckload is 40,000, then you can generate a reorder about every two weeks. This interval may change if the product is seasonal or if the popularity of the product is changing.

During any given period, it may take more or less time to reach the reorder amount, but as long as the difference is not substantial, the figure given to the computer is no problem. If, however, you find that it is consistently taking more or less time to reach the reorder amount, then it may be time to change the order frequency in the computer for that vendor.

Reorder Frequency – Not Constrained 4.2.2

On occasion, a vendor will place no constraints on the size of the order. Theoretically, you could order every day or even twice a day. Actually, if there were no offsetting issues, ordering every day would be very desirable and would result in outstanding inventory performance. After all, most of the product would be in the pipeline, and the system would be able to respond to changes in demand almost instantly.

In actual practice, you would probably run into problems processing and handling the constant stream of relatively small orders. Accordingly, I suggest that you pick some reasonable review cycle, but no longer than one week. With the system we are developing, reviewing a vendor once a week is not difficult or time-consuming. Generally, a reorder can be generated in ten to twenty minutes for even the largest vendor.

Lead Times 4.3

Lead time is not just the time it takes the vendor to ship the order. It is the time from when the order is initiated to when the product is ready for shipment to a customer. In fact, the lead time should be extended even more if the data is less than current at the time of ordering, which could occur if data is being sent in from outlying locations.

We are interested in the future lead time, not the past. Generally, the two are the same, but there will be occasions when a vendor encounters a new situation that causes his delivery times to change. Certain times of the year create bottlenecks with certain suppliers that, in turn, translate into longer response times. In other cases, longer response times may be result from work stoppages or facility problems. Building a replenishment order based on historic tracking of lead times — while not catastrophic to the system — will be less effective than basing the order on current data. .

Since the new system we are formulating is going to relieve the purchasing manager of 95 percent of the "dog work," it is reasonable to expect that he or she will now use some of this freed time to communicate more effectively with suppliers and, in turn, be aware of critical factors such as changed lead times.

4.3.1 Lead Times – SKU Level vs. Vendor Level

Much confusion exists over the issue of whether lead times are all the same. Normally, all the lead times of the SKUs you are addressing for a single order have the same lead time by definition. You are building a purchase order for a group of items that are all going to arrive on the same truck, or as part of a specific shipment. The fact that some of these items will be back-ordered, and will arrive at a later date, is academic. We do not know in advance which items will be late; they simply become part of the statistical "noise" of the system to be covered by the safety stock. (Incidentally, if the vendor is notorious for having massive back-orders which cause over half the order to arrive at different dates, then I would use a lead time that is an approximation of when about 80 percent of the product can be expected to arrive.)

If the more unusual situation arises, where different predictable lead times are co-mingled in the same restocking order, then it is necessary to have the system recognize that each SKU has its own stated lead time. This is cumbersome, however, since it means that to maintain the records we must have the ability to change each SKU individually. On the other hand, if the lead times are set at the vendor level, we can arrange to have the system change lead times with a single entry for the entire group of SKUs. Be sure you truly understand your own situation; do not automatically assume that there are different lead times for each item — it may not be the case!

Incidentally, I have run into situations where people have been convinced that they had two separate groups of lead times; the reality was that the vendor was shipping from two separate points. Consequently, the purchase orders could have been built independently with common lead times per order.

Building a Restocking Order

Now that we have a series of techniques for developing an excellent forecast and reorder target, we need to blend these techniques into a software system that will allow us to interact with the system to build a purchase order against a vendor.

In this section, we will outline the process for building the system, which we will refer to as "demand forecasting." Characteristics and features of the system are:

1. It will organize all the required information on a single series of screens for easy access and review. Moreover, additional screens for additional detail information will "pop up" on command with a simple keystroke.

2. It will *automatically* make a recommended inventory restock purchase order, but will allow us to interact in areas where we have special information not known to the computer (e.g., special one-time promotions, unusual demands that have been communicated to us outside the system, etc.).

3. It will deal with roughly 95 percent of the items *automatically*, but it will also invite us to review data where sales patterns indicate that something might benefit from human review.

4. It will deal with the great variety of "real world" problems we run into in the distribution business, such as minimum order amounts, palletizing requirements, economic order quantity (EOQ) considerations, special buys, etc.

This software package will allow us to sit down at the computer and develop a replenishment purchase order on a specific vendor in less than fifteen minutes. This replenishment order will comprehend changes in demand levels, trends, and seasonality. It will also balance to full-truckload requirements or other minimum order restraints. And finally, despite the speed of processing, it will be the best reorder you can imagine, putting the right item in the right place at the right time!

This is the system we will now outline.

5.1   Identifying the Correct Group of SKUs

Before we can start to build an order, it is necessary for the primary accounting software to "gather up" the SKUs that relate to the particular vendor and warehouse we wish to restock. With this information, we can then address all the SKUs provided by the vendor (or a specific warehouse of the vendor) that are utilized by one of our warehouses (or group of warehouses that can be replenished by the same purchase order).

Almost any modern computerized distribution system will track the on-hand balances and sales history of our "authorized stock items." Moreover, the software will allow us, via various codes and selection criteria, to extract these records into a working file.

At this point, the computer should calculate the forecast and the reorder target for each SKU in the file (as we have outlined in the preceding sections), and display the results on a reorder screen, as shown in exhibit G. This exhibit is only the first "page" of the potential reorder and, at this point, contains features we have not yet discussed.

(Note: From this point forward, we will talk about the computer output and features as if they exist. As I mentioned earlier, a number of systems have been designed along the concepts I have developed, and they operate almost exactly as described in our discussion. Alternatively, you can program these concepts into your system by following the described methodology.)

At this point, I will demonstrate how easily an order can be produced, and how the computer can perform the "lion's share" of the work, while still giving us the opportunity to intervene to interject special considerations known only to us.

Exhibit G is an example of a reordering screen.

The item numbers are the stock numbers of the SKUs that have come up for potential reordering. On the screen, we have a series of columns that I will elaborate on later. For the moment, we are going to focus on the middle column called "NORM" (normal). This is the amount we want to order, based on the reorder target we discussed earlier (in Section 3.0). The circled number 14 tells us to order 14 units of item 75GMF5.

Exhibit G

Build An Order

Vendor: 070440   GNB, Inc.

Item#	Loc.	Avail.	On Ord.	Low	Norm.	High	Max	Sugg	Flags
22NFG2	1	4	4	2	2	4	5	2	
27LTHD5	1	11	18	0	3	5	7	3	
27FLTHD5	1	9	7	2	6	8	14	6	
34CH5	1	21	6	0	4	9	13	4	
34GMF5	1	17	0	4	8	12	16	8	
3EEG3	1	6	5	0	3	7	11	3	*
41dP5	1	4-	9	5	8	12	17	8	
42P5	1	0	8	4	7	11	14	7	
4DG900	1	46	0	0	0	12	27	0	
75GMF5	1	23	8	0	(14)	18	22	4	
78CH5	1	14	6	0	0	0	5	0	
8DG1150	1	175	36	18	36	36	72	36	P

	Cost	Grs. Wt.	Net Wt.	Volume	Quantity
Tots.	$42,176.62	33,146.00	00.00	00.00	942
Goal	.00	.00	.00	.00	0

O-Order Level	I Item Detail	C-Calcs
G-Goal Seeking	T-Toggle Zeros	P-Print

Enter-Chg. Qty.   F-Find By Item
L-Lock/Unlock   E-Exit

To understand how this figure came about, we can utilize another built-in feature of the system. When we hit a specially designated key, the system will overlay a screen (see Exhibit H) that shows the full detail background information about the item over which the highlighter is stationed. If we hit the key again, the overlay will disappear and put back to the original reorder screen.

We will use the overlay screen to discover how the system arrives at its reordering values; we will also use this screen on a routine basis to interact with the system and track items of special interest. Incidentally, this overlay screen is an ideal way for a purchasing manager to access additional backup information about a specific item under scrutiny. We are going to use the screen now, however, to discuss the design of the system.

In our example, let's assume the highlighter is over the third item from the bottom, item 75GMF5, which also has a circled NORM level of 14.

The screen in Exhibit H provides critical background information about the SKU in question. There is basic descriptive information, three years of sales history, stock status data, and finally key reorder information.

The reorder target is 41 units. Earlier, we said the amount to be reordered should be the reorder target less the sum of the amount on hand plus on order. In our example, the net stock is 27. The target is 41, and if we subtract 27 from 41, we

---

Exhibit H

Item Detail for : 75GM F5				Location: Minn.	
Description:			Automotive Battery - GNB Group Size 75 - 650 CCA		
Sales History					
Month	**1991**	**1992**	**1993**	**On Hand:**	**23**
Jul	45	65	71	**Committed:**	**4**
Aug	36	71	83	**Back Ordered:**	**0**
Sep	48	88	101	**On Order:**	**8**
Oct	74	83	92		
Nov	92	101	121	**Net:**	**27**
Dec	103	123	132		
Jan	89	106	120		
Feb	45	82	80		
Mar	48	76	82	**Months Supply:**	**.3**
Apr	21	85	92	**Forecast:**	**75**
May	52	93	101	**Reorder Target:**	**41**
Jun	49	92	34		

get a desired order amount of 14. Note that the figure under NORM in Exhibit G is, in fact, 14.

The system has repeated this calculation for every SKU, and the figures in the NORM column are the recommended reorder amounts for the products supplied by the vendor we called up.

Note: Not every SKU will come up on the screen. We will arrange to have the system bring up only those SKUs for which demand is at the MAX level. (MAX will be defined later; for the moment, visualize it as a higher level of forced demand.) This technique eliminates all the SKUs for which there is more-than-ample product on hand, thereby not cluttering up the screen. This feature has real pertinence for vendors with hundreds, if not thousands, of SKUs. My system saves the user from the tedious task of having to scan down a series of screens filled with endless zero requirements.

Even though the system will not bring up all SKUs automatically, it does have a feature that allows us to call up all SKUs — including those that were suppressed by the system because no demand was indicated at the MAX level. The system will interject all SKUs with one keystroke. This is handy if, during the order process, we start to wonder about a particular SKU that is not on the screen. After checking out the SKU in question, we then hit the same key as before and the screen reverts back to the original display.

This feature represents one of numerous techniques we are building into the system to make it easy to work with. It is part of the reason I am able to build a comprehensive purchase order within fifteen minutes from the time I sit down at the computer.

Creating the Order

To initiate the procedure to create an order, we hit the "O" key (in this particular system); the system then transfers all the figures under the NORM column to the SUGG (suggested) column at the right side of the screen. Simultaneously, the system calculates the total order being generated in terms of Cost, Gross Weight, Net Weight, Volume, and Quantity (as shown along the bottom of Exhibit G).

We are going to fine-tune the order in a number of ways, but at this point it is a valid order and theoretically could be turned into a bona fide purchase order without too much risk.

There is, a subjective way of looking at the figures in the NORM column. The system is saying to us:

> *"If you are going to order today, and are not going to order again for seven days, and if it takes 14 days for the product to arrive, and if the sales history and the seasonality are as stated, and if you want a certain fill level (such as 97 percent), then you want the reorder target units to be either on hand or in the pipeline. Accordingly, you should order the difference, which is called the NORM. If you are already over the target amount, then you do not have to order that item.*

> *Furthermore, if you order more than the NORM amount, it is excess; and if you order less, all bets are off for 97 percent fill."*

Having established the NORM order, we are ready to start taking some other factors into consideration.

The NORM order indicates quantities needed to satisfy normal demand for the product and to do so at a specific order fill level. As we are only too aware, other considerations, such as pallet quantities, carton restrictions, minimum order quantities, and economic order quantities, must be recognized and taken into account. These considerations may or may not cause us to override our original NORM quantities, but they need our attention. In the following chapters, I will illustrate how we can equip the system with the logic necessary to perform these functions automatically, with sophistication that we would be hard-pressed to duplicate manually.

Some products are subject to lot sizing or palletizing requirements (i.e., although the SKU is ordered and priced as "each," the vendor requires that the SKU be ordered in lots or pallets of a certain amount). If pallet sizes are mandatory, and we cannot buy the product in anything other than multiples of the lot size, then our decision is straightforward. After calculating the NORM, we simply round up to the next pallet size or lot size. If the lot size is 12, and the NORM calls for eight, the system will order 12; if the NORM calls for 18, the system will order 24.

Now let's deal with a more problematic situation. Let's assume, as is true in my business, that I can order individual passenger car batteries one at a time from my vendor, but it is more convenient to handle the batteries in pallets of 20 because they stack better in the truck, and I can use a forklift truck to load them into the racks. In this situation, I would probably round up to a full pallet if the NORM called for 15 or 18 items. After all, that is only an extra two or five units. However, if the NORM called for only seven items, I wouldn't want the additional 13 items. That would be almost twice what the system was calling for, and the extra inventory could not be justified to eliminate a partial pallet.

To effectively respond to vendor requirements, we will create a "Lot Sizing" variable that we specifically set for each SKU. If we set this variable at 100 percent, it will mean that lot sizing is mandatory and the system will automatically round up the NORM quantities to the next pallet or lot size. If we set our variable at some figure below 100 percent, to a level of let's say 40 percent, the system will check to see if the "extra" product required to reach a full pallet exceeds 40 percent of the original order. If so, the system will not round up. If the percentage of extra product required to reach a full pallet is less than 40, the system will round up.

By using percent as the criteria, the system will emulate the human judgment process beautifully, and will order pallet amounts only if the "extra" quantities are reasonable. For example, the system will order a pallet of 20 if the unconstrained reorder is for 17, but it will not go to a pallet of 20 if the NORM calls for eight. However, the system will go to five pallets of 20 if the NORM calls for 88. (The system will not accept an extra 12 units when the NORM only calls for eight, but it will accept an extra 12 units when the NORM calls for 88.) Isn't this what you would do if you were making manual adjustments?

By adjusting the "Lot Sizing" percent, we can affect the system's aggressiveness in going to a full pallet. For example, if the benefit of going to a full pallet is only stocking and handling convenience, then setting the Lot Sizing at 40 percent might be about right. However, if there is an economic incentive to palletizing (i.e., the vendor will give an extra one percent price discount if we order in pallet quantities), then we may want to set the Lot Sizing at 80 percent to more aggressively force a full pallet. Some simple trial and error experimenting will help you determine a reasonable level.

One additional point: Before deciding not to order an extra 12 units to get to a full pallet of 20, the system will make another check to see if the extra 12 units are less than 40 percent of a month's supply. If so, the system will go to the full pallet after all. This action is based on the logic that even if the extra amount is a fairly high percentage of the ordered amount, it may be a relatively small percent of the monthly sales.

Note that the system is mimicking what you would do if given unlimited time to contemplate each item, except that it does it automatically and consistently.

When we invoke the palletizing feature, we will place a "P" (for Palletizing) in the right hand column of the reorder screen under FLAG (as in the lower right hand corner of Exhibit G) so that the purchasing manager can see when the NORM was overridden.

With a little imagination, this optional palletizing feature can be used to meet a variety of additional vendor requirements that are not at first self-evident.

5.3.2 Minimum Order

In addition to lot sizing, some vendors require that an order of a particular SKU be at least X units. For example, we may be able to order in lots of 12, but the order for that SKU must be for at least 48 units. To address this situation, we will utilize a field in the SKU record that we can set to this minimum requirement. The system will then respond properly. If the unconstrained order is for 30 units, the system will order 48; if the unconstrained order is for 55, the system will order 60 (next lot size up).

Whenever we invoke this feature, we will place an "M" (for Minimum Order) in the right hand column of the reorder screen under FLAG. This flag is particularly important because of the rigorous nature of the constraint. For example, if the system wanted just one item, but the minimum was 100, then it would order the full 100. You, in turn, may decide that regardless of what the system wants and the vendor has decreed, you will do without this item.

Economic Order Quantity Calculations

In our earlier discussion of the "Reorder Target," I mentioned that at the time of building a restocking order, the system would reorder the difference between the "net available" and the "reorder target." Under certain circumstances, and particularly in certain industries, this approach could create reorder amounts for specific SKUs that are too small to justify the handling and stocking cost. To us, it would be intuitively obvious that rather than order the small amount the system is calling for, it would make better sense to reorder a larger amount and eliminate intermediate orders.

To deal with this situation, we will utilize a feature called the "Economic Order Quantity" (EOQ). This feature calculates how much more of a given SKU we should order to balance the cost of handling the product during restocking versus the added cost of carrying extra inventory. The EOQ feature can override the normal reorder system and increase the size of an order to eliminate the handling costs associated with frequent reordering of small quantities. In doing so, the EOQ feature recognizes that by ordering more product than the system wants for effective order fill purposes, it is incurring a cost of inventory holding.

The EOQ calculation will give us the best trade-off by assessing the costs of carrying extra inventory versus the cost savings realized by eliminating extra orders and their associated handling costs.

To fully understand the EOQ feature, we need to explore a series of concepts.

5.4.1   **Definition of Terms**

Two key numbers must be established before the system can calculate the EOQ. These numbers are the cost of initiating and handling a restock, and the cost of carrying inventory.

5.4.1.1   **Order Initiating and Handling Cost**

The order initiating and handling cost is the expense associated with the creation of an extra SKU on a purchase order, plus the expense associated with putting that quantity of the SKU on the shelves of the warehouse.

First of all, it is important to understand that this handling cost is the incremental (or out-of-pocket) cost of creating a reorder, processing it, and finally receiving the product and stocking it in the bins.

In today's computer environment, the incremental cost of creating an extra SKU on a purchase order is zero. The only incurred cost, therefore, is the cost of receiving the order and stocking it in the bins.

Obviously, a tremendous number of variables can influence the handling cost. The cost can be different due to conditions at the moment of restocking. If a series of items requiring restocking are all clustered in the same warehouse area and the bins are clear for easy restocking, the costs are far lower than if the items are spread all over the warehouse and the bins are in a state of disarray.

Accordingly, it is necessary to make a stab at a figure for handling costs; you can refine the figure after you've tried a few restocking simulations. I recommend that you start with a figure of one dollar. By doing so, you are assuming that the process of handling a single SKU incurs about one dollar of incremental cost. This figure is based on the assumption that the only real cost in putting away an item is the labor cost.

This figure may appear low and, in fact, is lower than suggested by many sources; but in my opinion, it is more valid than figures I have heard that are as high as five dollars. One dollar equates to about four minutes of labor when the base rate is $10 per hour ($10/hr is about equal to $15 when fringe costs are included. That equals 25¢/hr or $1.00 for four minutes).

Although it may take longer to handle some items, on other occasions three or more items may be put away at virtually the same time. Quite often the incremental cost of handling an item is zero anyway, since it is impractical to eliminate the cost even if the task is eliminated.

The people who recommend the five-dollar handling cost arrive at their figure by including many fixed costs that will not change regardless of how many items are being processed.

Don't get too hung up on this number. Treat it as an index that you can modify with experience. The key point is that the system will consistently respond to the figure you use and drive the size of orders for each item in a logical and consistent manner.

Carrying Cost

Carrying cost tells us how much it has cost us incrementally to keep the inventory around for the extra time period. The cost is expressed as a percentage; when multiplied by the value of the inventory, it provides the carrying cost in dollars. The components of this figure are:

a. The Cost of Money—This is the interest on the money tied up by the excess product. While interest rates are in a continuous state of flux, using 12 percent annually or one percent per month is a reasonable compromise.

b. Other Stocking Costs—Keeping product in inventory incurs costs in the categories of insurance, warehouse operations, obsolescence, and potential product damage. However, few of these costs are incremental. That is, few of these actions create an "out-of-pocket expense" or conversely will go away if we stock more or less inventory. Nevertheless, it is also dangerous to ignore these factors since, in the long run, non-incremental costs have a way of becoming truly incurred expenses. I recommend that you assume this grab bag of items is worth about another 0.5 percent per month.

The cost of money and the cost of stocking add up to a carrying cost of 1.5 percent per month or 18 percent per year. Again, don't get too hung up on these figures since, as indicated earlier, we are creating a mechanism that we can fine tune to get the system to follow our warehousing philosophy on a consistent and methodical basis.

The EOQ Calculation

Having established the definition of the two key numbers — the cost of initiating and handling an order, and the cost of carrying inventory —we are now in a position to calculate the Economic Order Quantity (EOQ). The calculation is as follows:

EOQ = Square Root of [(2 x C x FCST) / (PCT x CST)]

Where:

C	=	the cost of initiating and handling the order
FCST	=	the monthly forecast
PCT	=	the monthly percent carrying cost
CST	=	the product cost (or value)

Using some actual numbers:

C	=	$1.00
FCST	=	4
PCT	=	.015
CST	=	$5.00

EOQ = Square Root of [(2 x 1.00 x 4) / (.015 x 5.00)]
EOQ = Square Root of [8/.075]
EOQ = Square Root of [106.7]
EOQ = 10.3 or 10

In this example, the calculation is telling us that it is more economical to order 10 units, or a little over two months' supply of the item, instead of the three or four units the system wants for sales response. The cost of holding an extra two months' supply is offset by the item being handled only once during the period.

Incidentally, if the EOQ is more than a full year's supply, the system should automatically cut the order back to equal one year's supply. The rational behind this action resides in the fact that beyond one year we start to run into issues of product obsolescence and deterioration, which were not part of the original parameters.

In actual use, the EOQ feature will allow every SKU, regardless of its popularity, to be considered for restocking during the normal scheduled ordering period. If the item has fallen below the reorder target, the system will trigger a reorder. The reorder amount will be either the minimum required to get back to the reorder target, or the EOQ amount, whichever is larger. If the item has a fairly low value and forecast usage, the system will call for a larger reorder to eliminate frequent handling. The item will then stay off the reorder display for a considerable period. When the on-hand balance is depleted, the item will come up automatically for reordering consideration.

Note: By using this concept, we completely eliminate the need, proposed by other systems, to set individual artificial reorder time cycles based on the popularity of the individual SKU. The other approach again requires manual intervention to accomplish what the techniques we have been developing perform automatically with ease and accuracy. Additionally, when these other systems artificially put longer review cycles on products, they are unnecessarily increasing the inventory levels and lowering fill rates.

5.4.4 Fine Tuning the EOQ

As previously discussed, much of the "theoretical stuff" is shot through with questionable assumptions and should not be empowered with any assumption of precision. These theories do, however, provide us with a mechanism to drive our system in the direction we want.

Consequently, after setting up some initial parameters, you should build a trial order and scan it for reasonableness. By increasing "handling cost," you should notice that the system starts ordering larger amounts of the slower-moving, low-value items. Additionally, subsequent reorders will then tend to trigger fewer line items for reorder, since many candidates will be "overstocked" because the EOQ was activated during the prior cycle.

After a few cycles of ordering, it will become apparent if the system is reacting in a way that feels right to you and is matching your warehouse operating philosophy. Throughout this process, the important point is that the system is automatically tracking both the popular items and slow-moving items during every review period. In fact, even when a popular item changes to one that is less so, the system automatically responds.

5.4.5 The "Q" Flag

Whenever we invoke the EOQ feature, we will place a "Q" (for EOQ) in the right hand column of the reorder screen under FLAG. This will alert us to the fact that the system has increased the NORM reorder amount to a higher EOQ level. We will then know when the system ordered more than the normal quantity, and the reason for the override.

To this point, we have developed a system that will generate an order that comprehends a wide variety of issues such as palletizing, minimum order requirements, and EOQ considerations. This order could be turned into a bona fide purchase order, and it would do a respectable job of bringing in the right product at the right time in the right quantity. While it lacks the special input a human might have in certain circumstances, the system has built-in safeguards to keep it from doing "dumb" things. Moreover, the system's EOQ and palletizing features have enhanced the initial order, without human intervention, to make it even closer to the requirements of the real world.

The order does lack one very critical element, however — the special knowledge and wisdom of a human who may be aware of certain things a statistical system simply couldn't know. So, at this point, I want to introduce some features that allow the human to interact with the system and provide the manual overrides that start to optimize the unique features of both the computer and the human.

The need for human override can result from a variety of reasons, and we will introduce techniques to facilitate each.

Overriding a Single Item   6.1

At times, you will want to insert your own reorder amount for a specific SKU. Perhaps a salesperson has just sold an extraordinary quantity of product that has yet to be entered into the system. Whatever the reason, let's assume that an override is necessary. The "arbitrary override" can be accomplished by moving the highlighter bar down to the item, hitting the enter key, entering the new quantity, and then hitting the enter key again. When the second "enter" stroke is made, all the quantities along the bottom of the screen will change to reflect the impact of the manual intervention.

Whenever we invoke the arbitrary override, we will place an "L" in the right hand column of the reorder screen under FLAG. This will indicate that the quantity is now "locked," and will not change when we trigger other features in the system.

6.2 Overriding a Group of Items

On other occasions, you may want to increase the reorder amount on a group of items. Perhaps a promotion not comprehended in the seasonal indices is taking place. The procedure for overriding the system is identical to the one we just followed in Section 6.1., and numerous items can be changed in seconds. In this situation, however, we will want to provide some statistical guidance regarding the amounts to be ordered. This can be accomplished by developing another feature into the system that uses the columns in Exhibit G marked LOW, HIGH, and MAX.

These added columns of LOW, HIGH, and MAX have a variety of uses. Conceptionally, the columns are statistically modified levels of reordering that display a spectrum of demands. They give the user a variety of ordering levels that are statistically sound, and insure that any overrides of the NORM will not create serious inventory out-of-balance problems.

To create the LOW, HIGH, and MAX levels, simply recalculate the "reorder target," but use a multiplier on the assumed lead time (e.g., for HIGH, use 1.2 times the lead time and then calculate the reorder target). The amount of the reorder is then the "available" less the target. This technique statistically increases the demand, but in proportion to the forecast. Incidentally, because the multipliers are "user determined," the spread of the columns can be varied.

A benefit of this approach is that we are made aware of items that did not require any product at the NORM level, but do have a requirement at either the HIGH or MAX level. This is because the item was on the verge of being needed at the normal level, but did not quite hit the target. Once we kick up the lead time, the item becomes a candidate for restocking.

The LOW, HIGH, and MAX columns can be utilized for a variety of manual overrides. Let's assume you are going to run a promotion on a series of twelve SKUs and you want to "hype" the reorder for this group of items. In this situation, the extra columns will provide some guidance in determining how much you should increase each item within the group and yet keep the items in balance with each other. Start by selecting the column that "feels best," and transfer these values into the SUGG column. By doing this, you will achieve the "hype" called for by the special promotion, but you will be fairly certain that you have kept the items in proportion to each other relative to their forecast.

Overriding Due to Computer Prompting

We will now add a feature which prompts the computer to track sales history and call our attention to patterns or trends that may be of special interest to us. It will spot out-of-the-ordinary situations where we may have some special insights the computer lacks.

The system will alert us to these overrides by placing an asterisk in the FLAG column (see Exhibit G, the sixth item down, 3EEG3).

Three situations should cause the system to trigger an asterisk:

a. Earlier we discussed the creation of the MAD (Mean Average Deviation), which is a measure of the variability of the sales history, and also the deseasonalized average, which is a measure of the fundamental level of the demand.

If we use the ratio of the MAD to the deseasonalized average — and trigger an asterisk if the ratio is greater than one — we will have an excellent indicator of data that represents highly erratic patterns, and therefore raises questions. It is interesting how, in actual practice, this technique will effectively spot sales patterns that truly represent some special situation (e.g., sudden loss of a major customer, a radical increase in popularity, etc.).

Columns A through C of Exhibit I provide examples of sales data that would be flagged with an asterisk due to their ratio being above one. Column A might represent a situation in which a major customer ordered 20 units back in January and was running acceptability tests for five months before starting to order on a regular basis. This is something only a human would know. The system will, however, alert the user, who then can decide whether or not to override the system as an exception.

Column B is a case where sales of the product were brisk and then dropped off rapidly the last two months. This might have been due to a rapid shift in demand stimulated by a better, newly introduced substitute; or it might have been that the the vendor was chronically out of stock the last two months, and we were unable to ship. In either case, the system will alert us with an asterisk, thereby enabling us to recognize the real world situation and override the computer.

Column C is the reverse of Column B. In this case, the demand took off radically in the last two months, indicating that something was happening in the market that might call for an override of the inventory order.

Incidentally, you can set the ratio to make the trigger more or less sensitive. Be careful, however, because, as usual, there are trade-offs. If the trigger is made more sensitive, it will spot subtle movements, but it will also fill the screen with asterisks that mean nothing.

Exhibit I

Types of Sales Data that Will Trigger an Asterisk

Month	Product A	Product B	Product C	Product D	Product E
Jul	0	35	54	67	0
Aug	0	36	45	71	0
Sep	0	41	58	59	0
Oct	0	27	63	69	0
Nov	0	37	72	57	0
Dec	0	50	49	80	0
Jan	20	48	68	83	0
Feb	0	34	52	78	0
Mar	0	29	42	69	0
Apr	0	32	52	58	0
May	0	28	69	452	0
Jun	21	3	102	81	17
Jul	24	0	113	73	21

b. We will trigger the asterisk if the system invokes the "filter" feature (see Section 2.2.4). A good example is Column D of Exhibit I where the 452 in May was filtered. The purpose of the asterisk here is to alert the user to the fact that the history contained a spike, which was filtered out. With this information, the user can either ignore the information (since the filter will keep the system from making a major inventory reorder error) or manually intervene.

c. We will trigger the asterisk if the forecast is based on three or less months of data (as shown in the last column of Exhibit I). The purpose of the asterisk here is to alert the user to the fact that the forecast for this item may be suspect, since it is based on fairly thin history. Again, you can decide the number of months that will trigger this feature, but three seems to make sense.

Although the asterisk invites you to manually override the system, it does not necessarily mean you should. In actual practice, I have frequently found that I was comfortable with the way the computer handled the data, despite the data's apparent instability.

Forcing an Order to Reach a Minimum Load

The last method for overriding the initial reorder level has to do with the need to order up to minimum loads.

At this point, we have built an order based on the system's criteria to drive for maximum turns within desired order fill levels. We also have modified the order to comprehend pallet and EOQ considerations plus a series of factors outside the computer providence. If the total order size is satisfactory, we can proceed to cut a purchase order and move on to the next vendor.

Let's assume, however, that the order comes up short of the minimum amount needed to take advantage of discounts or prepaid freight. We still have two effective ways to manipulate the order, both based on statistical criteria. (Section 8.0 more fully discusses conditions that dictate when a reorder should be forced.)

Using the LOW, HIGH, and MAX Columns

One order override technique utilizes the HIGH and MAX columns introduced earlier in Section 6.2. The system should be programmed so that we can position the highlighter over either of these two columns. Once the enter key is punched, the figures in the selected column are transferred to the SUGG column, with the totals of Weight, Cost, Units, etc. modified accordingly. Note: items with "locked" quantities will not be changed.

The net effect of this feature will be to transfer what was in the HIGH or MAX columns, except for the locked items, into the SUGG column, and then display the new order totals below. This may bring the totals close to where you want them, and with some fine tuning, you have your order where you want it.

The range of the spread of the four columns (LOW, NORM, HIGH, and MAX) is determined by a set of "multipliers" that artificially increase the lead time, which in turn drives the reorder target. These multipliers should be set at default levels of .8 for LOW, 1.0 for NORM, 1.2 for HIGH, and 1.5 for MAX. As discussed earlier in Section 6.2, we arrive at the reorder target for the MAX by using a lead time that is artificially increased by a factor of 1.5.

If you find you are not getting sufficient spread in the columns, you can increase the HIGH and MAX multipliers. If you find that it takes a multiplier much in excess of the 1.5 to reach a full truckload, I would question the wisdom of forcing an order to these levels.

Goal Seeking

There is another technique that we can use to force an order to a level other than the NORM would dictate. We can create a feature which we will call "Goal Seeking." To use the goal seeking feature, follow this sequence of steps:

1. Hit some appropriate function key. The system will then prompt you to select the criterion which determines a full order (e.g., units, dollars, pounds, etc.).

2. Position the highlighter over the appropriate criterion.

3. After highlighting the appropriate criterion, key in the amount towards which you want the system to drive. (i.e., If your reorder must hit a full truckload — which is 40,000 pounds — you would select weight as the criterion and then key in 40,000 as the objective.)

5. The system will now make extensive calculations to increase or decrease the order to meet your "goal." To accomplish this, the system will artificially modify the lead time to statistically drive the size of the order in the desired direction. Additionally, the process will be iterative (repeated) since we are not going to be able to drive directly to the desired answer in one set of calculations. The system will make one attempt, and then stop and ask if you are satisfied with the solution. If you are not, you simply request another iteration and the system will drive in on the goal to a tighter degree.

   Generally it will take two to three iterations before the system gets close enough. The system will rarely hit the goal exactly, since we are not dealing with what is mathematically called a "continuous function." Consequently, once you are close enough to the goal, it is a simple matter to clean up the last few units with the override process.

To build the goal seeking feature into the demand forecasting system, we will need to take the following steps:

1. To start, we will need to program the system with a multiplier of the lead time that is a "first approximation." Since we have nothing to give us guidance at this point, we will arbitrarily start with a multiplier of 1.5. The objective here is to give the system a chance to find out how much the load changes for a given change in lead time. Having "learned" from this transaction, the system will then adjust the lead time for a second shot.

2. Using the 1.5 multiplier, the system will recalculate the reorder target and the amount of product to be ordered for every SKU in the file, including SKUs that did not come up in the original order. The system will also make all determinations regarding the EOQ and palletizing. At the end of this process, the system will display the totals for each criterion of the order. (e.g., At this point, the order might read 47,345 pounds. — The system overshot the 40,000 we were after.)

3. Now, by taking the amount (in pounds) by which the order was increased, and comparing it to the percent by which we increased the lead time, we can calculate how much to modify the next lead time multiplier for the second iteration. We then repeat step two, using the new lead time.

4. Step three can be repeated as frequently as necessary, always using the new relationships of lead time to results. As you can see, with each iteration we get closer and closer to the final desired result.

This process can take quite a few minutes, depending on the number of SKUs being considered. With each iteration, the system is checking each and every SKU in the system to determine if that SKU can statistically contribute to the objective. The final solution insures that the added product is distributed across the remaining SKUs in such a manner that the SKUs have a uniform probability of being consumed. Stated differently, the extra product has been distributed to provide the maximum added protection for each SKU.

We tend to talk about adding extra product to meet a minimum order requirement because this is the most common situation. The technique of goal seeking is just as powerful in the reverse situation (i.e., if we have to artificially reduce an order). Let's say we want to limit the reorder to a specific dollar amount below the quantity called for by the system. In this case, the system will take out the extra product in a manner the minimizes the adverse impact on future expected order fill.

Product Allocation Between Warehouses

In a perfect environment, each warehouse would have just the right items, at just the right time, to take care of its own needs with no excess stock. In the real world, however, the normal unpredictability of future demand will create dislocations of stock, to say nothing of customer returns, cancelled orders, etc.

Our system, therefore, must contain tools to handle this periodic need to rebalance stocking locations. The issue of dislocated or unbalanced stock arises in three distinct situations. Let's look at each in turn.

7.1 **Out-of-Stock Crises**

The first situation which might drive product allocation arises in the order entry phase (or inquiry phase) of your regular accounting software system. Let's assume that your order entry operator enters an order only to discover that the local shipping point is out of stock; there is a potential here for a lost sale. At this point, we need to program a feature into the system, so that by hitting an appropriate function key, a screen will appear (as in Exhibit J).

This screen is comprised of elements of data that are either basic to the primary accounting system or basic to the inventory management system we are discussing. The only exception is the "Months Supply On Hand," which is the on-hand balance divided by the forecast. (If seasonality exists, and we want this figure to accurately reflect inventory balances, we should "simulate" the months before the balance will be consumed. This can be done by subtracting the coming seasonally adjusted forecast from the on-hand balance, and if there is product remaining, subtracting the next seasonally adjusted forecast from the remainder, etc.)

"Excess Units" is the amount of product in excess of a supply previously specified for a certain number of months, such as three. For example, in Exhibit J there are 33 units in the PT warehouse; the forecast is for 5 units per month, so a three months' supply is 15; 33 minus 15 is 18 excess units.

A quick scan of the screen will immediately tell us where the opportunities for reallocation lie. In Exhibit J it is clear that the third location — PT — has excess stock available for use at the location needing stock. However, even if no excess stock exists, if a sale is in jeopardy, the operator might elect to pull stock from a location that is reasonably balanced, but has stock for rapid cross-shipment. The number of variables and degrees of subjective judgement required at this point are considerable. The key is to provide the decision-maker with enough information to make a good decision. This screen accomplishes this objective.

Exhibit J

Product Allocation Advisory
Product Code: AS1957514

Location	Quantity On Hand	Quantity On Order	Forecast	Months Supply O.H.	Excess Units
AZ	0	23	12	0.0	0
MS	12	0	14	.9	0
PT	33	0	5	6.7	18

7.2   Transshipment at Time of Reordering

The next situation which might drive product allocation arises during the reordering phase. If excess stock exists for a particular SKU at some other location, a "#" sign will appear in the FLAG column on the far right of the ordering screen. When the operator hits the appropriate function key, the screen shown earlier will reappear. The operator then needs to decide whether to use stock from the other location in lieu of reordering on the vendor.

When deciding between reallocating and ordering, it is important to determine whether the cost of shipping product from one location to another is offset by the utilization of product that might otherwise sit idle. We could get very technical here and develop a complex formula that relates these two variables for every combination of location in the system. The number of variables would become unmanageable very quickly, however, if we took into account issues such as the size of the transshipment (which determines the freight cost per dollar of product being shipped), the handling cost, the type of product, etc.

I have a "rule of thumb" which simplifies the decisionmaking process and is adequate for most purposes. My years of experience have led me to conclude that inventory generally costs about two percent per month and freight generally runs from three to six percent of the product value. Consequently, any product that is in excess of three months supply is an excellent candidate for reallocation.

Another point that substantiates this simple rule is that excess stock tends to be "either/or." That is, it either is in reasonable balance, or it tends to be way up in the six or more months supply level. Not too much stock falls into the "gray" zone, particularly if ordered by the demand forecasting system we are designing.

The final situation which might drive product allocation is the periodic need to do a complete inventory analysis to see if product should be reallocated between locations regardless of the reordering phase. The rationale for periodic reallocation is that it is more economical to transship all out-of-balance product at one time to minimize shipping expense rather than to transship on an item-by-item basis.

Obviously, inventory balancing alternatives are driven by the unique characteristics of each individual company. If the company has trucks periodically going between locations, then the cost of transfer is virtually zero, and the item-by-item approach makes sense. If, however, each item must bear its own shipping cost, then it may make more sense to do an overall review once every few months.

The product type also has a major bearing on which inventory management technique to use. If the item is high in value, but low in weight and volume, then frequent rerouting is practical and cost-effective. Rerouting heavier, low value items, conversely, is impractical and expensive.

The periodic review of inventory can be accomplished on the computer by creating a "Product Reallocation Report." This report lists any SKUs for which there is excess supply in at least one warehouse location. Exhibit K illustrates a sample product reallocation report. Note that all the SKUs of one type are grouped together so that it is immediately apparent which products can be efficiently transferred to alternate locations.

Exhibit K

Prod. Code	Description	Loc.	Quantity O.H.	O.O.	FCST	Month Supply	Excess Units
24LTHD5	GP24 Battery	AZ	28	0	4	6.5	14
24LTHD5	GP24 Battery	MS	2	0	2	.9	0
24LTHD5	GP24 Battery	PT	1	14	8	.1	0
27GMF5	GP27 Battery	AZ	76	14	56	1.3	0
27GMF5	GP27 Battery	MS	0	23	18	.0	0
27GMF5	GP27 Battery	PT	19	0	4	4.8	8

8.0   When to Reorder

In Section 4.2, we discussed "Reorder Frequency" and covered the various factors that drive us to set the reorder frequency to a specific level. For example, if we can generate a full truckload roughly every two weeks, then our order frequency is two weeks.

Reorder frequency is an objective rather than an absolute, since it is not critical that we reorder at exactly this frequency. This is true even though we put a specific time frequency into the system. We are, after all, dealing with a statistical system that has a certain amount of flexibility.

I will now elaborate on when we should initiate a restocking order.

8.1   Fixed Schedule

Some businesses need to reorder on a highly fixed schedule, in exact compliance with the interval given to the system. You and I might find ourselves in this situation for a variety of reasons:

a. We may be locked into a reorder cycle by the vendor, and have no choice.

b. We may be so busy coping with numerous vendors and SKUs that we want to set a schedule and hold to it regardless of what the reorder calls for at the moment, just to be able to deal with the workload.

With a fixed reordering schedule, the ability of the demand forecasting system to adjust the order to meet various vendor restrictions is invaluable. For example, if we create an order at the appointed time, and the order comes up short of the required quantity, then the goal seeking feature, or the extra columns of HIGH and MAX, can drive us to the desired level.

Incidentally, if you are finding that it takes more and more forcing to reach the required reorder quantity, it is time to consider skipping a reorder cycle. Keep in mind that the amount of product the system is ordering after the first pass at the NORM level is all the product the system needs to meet your demand requirements. Everything added to the NORM order is extra unneeded inventory that will incur added expense.

In other businesses, there may be no artificial constraints for triggering a restocking order. In this case, we simply want to optimize the system in terms of avoiding excess stock, while being sensitive to impending stock-outs. Following is one technique for deciding when to cut an order if the number of vendors you have is not overwhelming.

a. Attempt to build an order a few days prior to the scheduled reorder date. If the system builds to the critical quantity at the NORM level, you are home free. Cut the order and go! (This is not a time-consuming process, incidentally. It should be clear by now that the demand forecasting system we have created will very quickly arrive at an initial order.)

b. If the system didn't build to an order, keep trying each day until the system reaches the critical amount on its own. In parallel to this process, run a daily "Hot List" (see Section 9.3) to highlight potential out-of-stock situations. This report will alert you if you are running out of some sensitive items — which may override the issue of stock optimization.

c. Eventually one of two things will happen. Either you will automatically reach a reorder, or you will decide that you can't wait because some items are approaching critical inventory levels as highlighted by the "Hot List." If you can't wait until the system calls for a full reorder on its own, you are then in a position to "force" the order by using the techniques discussed in Section 6.4.

The process of trying to build an order every day may sound tedious and time-consuming. Keep in mind, however, that it takes only a few minutes to build an order on the first try when you are not incorporating manual overrides.

Another order-building option exists if you are dealing with a vast number of vendors and the method outlined above is impractical. It is possible to have the computer automatically run a broad range of vendors during the night. You can program the system so that it will attempt to build an order at the NORM level for each vendor. In the morning, the system will inform you of which vendors came within a certain percentage of reaching the critical reorder amount (the amount set in the "order objective quantity," which could be a figure such as 40,000 pounds). You then can select the percentage at which you want to see a run (e.g., 80 percent). With this input, the system will tell you which vendors reached the NORM level of 32,000 pounds or more (80 percent of 40,000). The system-generated orders for the identified vendors can then be recalled for final determination.

9.0   Management Reports

Up to this point, our entire discussion has focused on the process of building an optimum reorder in the most effective and efficient manner. Another critically important aspect of inventory management revolves around the use of management reports. These reports are "action reports" in the sense that they pinpoint specific areas requiring action. They also are exception-oriented, isolating the areas calling for action and omitting extraneous information.

We will utilize three management reports in the demand forecasting system: the Slow-Moving Report and the Hot List Report, which focus on specific details of SKUs; and the Profile Report, which is an overview or macro report.

9.1   Profile Report

A classic measurement of overall inventory effectiveness is the number of turns being achieved. While this figure can be a fair indication of the general health of an inventory, it fails to comprehend the overall makeup of the inventory on an item-by-item basis.

For example, an inventory could have 12 turns which, on the surface, is a fairly respectable performance. However, further analysis may show that half the inventory items have infinite turns but are chronically out of stock, while the other half is dead stock having zero turns. Obviously, despite the favorable-looking level of turns, the inventory is a disaster.

The situation is analogous to the man who drowned in a river that was only an average of four feet deep. Unfortunately, it was twelve feet deep in the middle!

In contrast to the measurement of "inventory turns," the "Profile Report" provides a meaningful and powerful overview of an inventory's composition and highlights any areas which should be analyzed in greater detail.

By posting warning signs, the Profile Report helps you avoid dangerous "drop-offs" when you're wading through rivers of SKUs. The report is a set of frequency distributions that slot each SKU into its range of months supply. It can be a little tricky to understand, but it provides an unequaled quick overview of the composition of an inventory and enables you to recognize and address the unseen and more subtle problems of inventory balance.

As we discussed earlier, the system maintains a demand forecast for each SKU. With this forecast, it is possible to calculate how many months supply of inventory exists for each particular item. The Profile Report utilizes the months supply figure to demonstrate how each SKU fits into a range of months supply, thereby establishing a profile of the inventory distribution.

To fully understand the Profile Report, we must study the sample report in Exhibit L.

Exhibit L

Profile Report

Month Supply			Item Count	Unit Count	Inventory Dollars
Zero Supply			4	0	$ 0
.1	to	.5	12	234	7.020
.6	to	1.0	62	1484	43,456
1.1	to	1.5	37	838	23,568
1.6	to	2.0	15	321	9,789
2.1	to	3.0	9	127	3,432
3.1	to	4.0	3	45	1,034
4.1	to	5.0	1	9	256
5.1	to	6.0	3	52	1,263
6.1	to	7.0	0	0	0
7.1	to	8.0	2	14	376
8.1	to	9.0	0	0	0
9.1	to	10.0	0	0	0
10.1	to	11.0	1	28	334
11.1	to	12.0	0	0	0
12.1	&	Over	8	03	748
	Total		160	3231	$91,276

This Profile Report is for a single vendor or for a defined group of products we wish to monitor. The totals indicate that this group of products is made up of 160 individual SKUs, comprised of 3,231 units, and worth $91,276. The SKUs are distributed by their individual months supply. For example, only one SKU had a months supply that was between 10.1 and 11.0 and it contained 28 units worth $334.

Let's define more fully each of the columns in the Profile Report.

1. The MONTHS SUPPLY column contains the monthly ranges into which each SKU will be slotted. The first range is Zero Supply; items in this range are out of stock. The second range is from 0.1 to 0.5; for items in this range, we have enough

inventory on hand to satisfy demand for one-tenth to one-half month. For items in the 12.1 and Over category, we have more than one year's supply on hand.

2. The ITEM COUNT column indicates the number of SKUs that fall into each months supply level. For example, only one SKU fell between 10.1 to 11.0 months supply, while 12 were between 0.1 to 0.5.

3. The UNIT COUNT tells how many units of the SKU fall into each months supply category. For example, 12 SKUs fell into the 0.1 to 0.5 range, and those 12 SKUs contained 234 units. The one SKU that fell into the 10.1 to 11.0 range had 28 units in stock.

4. The INVENTORY DOLLARS column shows the dollar amounts invested at each level of months supply. For example, we have more than a 12-month supply of eight SKUs; the 83 total units on hand cost us $748.

Note how quickly the full inventory picture unfolds. The very attractive Profile Report in our example is for a product line that has been running under the demand forecasting system for some time. Only four items are out of stock ("zero supply"), and only $748 is in the very slow-moving category (12.1 & over). Most of the stock is clustered between the 0.1 through 1.5 range, which is where inventory makes the most efficient contribution.

When a Profile Report is run for an inventory that has been under a loose manual system, the report inevitably has a very different look. Often a quarter of the items are out of stock, a third or more are over 12 months supply, and the rest are scattered throughout the other ranges.

Using the Profile Report

A Profile Report can be run for any vendor or group of vendors to check, at a glance, the overall composition of the inventory. Even if total turns look good for the product group, the Profile Report will isolate hidden problem areas for exploration.

If you run a Profile Report for a particular vendor, and a large number of SKUs appear in the 12-and-over months supply range, you may want to know which items have fallen into that category and why. To explore this issue so that detailed discussions can occur with the appropriate product manager, you should produce a "Slow-Moving Report."

Slow-Moving Report

The "Slow-Moving Report," as its name implies, lists the SKUs that are in excess supply. To create this report, we will have the system isolate the SKUs based on the number of months supply on hand rather than on the age of the product, which is a typical approach. With this method, items can appear on the report even though the inventory is made up of fresh stock from a manufacturer. A system that triggers slow-moving based on age allows the product to sit around for an extended period of time before finally deciding that it is slow moving.

Product returns or special orders rejected by the customer after receipt are classic examples of how we could end up with slow-moving product that was nevertheless fresh. Why wait around for six or eight months before deciding these products are a problem requiring action?

Referring back to the Profile Report in Exhibit L, we might find it interesting to know more about the eight items for which we had more than a twelve-month supply on hand. To analyze these eight items, we will have the system allow us to set the selection criteria so that only items with over twelve months supply are extracted and printed. A sample of this report is shown in Exhibit M.

Exhibit M

Slow Moving Exception Report
DSM Demo Company

All Items over 12.0 Months supply
Vendor: Grebner Batteries

			(A)	(B)	(C)	(D)	(E)
Wh	Item Number	Item Description	Stat	On Hand	On/Ord	Frcst	Mo Sply
01	24FGMF4	Battery, wet	12	17	0	-0	99.9
01	24FGMF4S	Battery, wet	12	34	0	3	15.1
01	24GMF3	Battery, wet	0	6	0	0	99.9
01	27FGMF5	Battery, wet	12	28	0	3	11.7
01	8DG1150S	Battery, wet	11	13	0	1	16.7
01	AG16TF590	Battery, wet	11	8	0	1	14.4
01	AG4EH940	Battery, wet	10	17	0	1	22.9
01	AP22NF	Battery, wet	12	18	0	0	99.9

The first three columns in the report give descriptive information about the selected items. The remaining column headings are as follows:

STAT (A) is the number of months the SKU has existed in the system. Its purpose is to warn us about items that are relatively new and therefore may not be truly slow-moving. The third item down, for example, has been in the system for zero months, which means it is a new SKU, not just newly arrived product, and not necessarily slow-moving.

ON HAND (B) is the on-hand balance of the SKU less the number of units already committed. This is the actual count of the inventory.

ON/ORD (C) is the amount of product on order; it is particularly critical to spot items for which product is on order when the current balance is in excess supply. This sounds unbelievable, but it does happen.

FRCST (D) is the demand forecast for the SKU.

MO/SPLY (E) is the months supply on hand for the SKU. This is the criterion by which the SKU is selected for the Slow-Moving Report. The figure is calculated by simulating the use of the item each month, recognizing the seasonality of the product.

The most important benefit of the Slow-Moving Report is the specific information it gives a manager. Rather than dealing in broad generalities, the manager can communicate to-the-point with the purchasing manager on specific issues. If there are no problems to pursue, the report makes it rapidly apparent, and the manager's time can be directed to more important areas.

Hot List Report

A conventional hot list is typically a list of all items which are out of stock. Once an item is out of stock, however, it is too late to do anything about it. Yet to ask a system to print out items when the balance is below some fixed figure can also be useless, since for one product an on-hand balance of ten may be dangerously low, while for another product, ten could be a month's supply.

In the demand forecasting system, the "Hot List" singles out items whose inventory levels are precariously low. The reports we generate with our system will be based on the months supply figure maintained by the system for each SKU. These reports will deal in days supply rather than months supply because we are concerned with items that are on the verge of being out of stock. Again we want to allow the user to establish the level at which the system will select the data. Typically you would be looking for items where the supply is below ten or fifteen days.

Following is a Hot List Report drawn from the Grebner Batteries inventory. The format is identical to the Slow-Moving Report, but the items listed are fast-moving rather than slow-moving.

Hot List Exception Report
DSM Demo Company
All Items Under 10 Days Supply
Vendor: Grebner Batteries

Wh	Item Number	Item Description	Stat	On Hand	On Order	Frcst	Days Supply
01	12N954B	Battery Fluid	12	-6	24	9	0
01	14LA2	Battery Fluid	12	4	20	17	7
01	18G	Battery, wet	12	-1	12	4	0
01	1G585	Battery, wet	12	-8	100	36	0
01	22NFG2	Battery, wet	12	-5	38	14	0
01	26RHE40	Battery, wet	12	0	4	2	0
01	29NFG3	Battery, wet	12	0	14	6	0
01	41P5	Battery, wet	12	6	36	24	8
01	65CH5	Battery, wet	11	0	40	5	0
01	78GMF5	Battery, wet	12	0	26	14	0
01	7DG940	Battery, wet	12	4	16	16	8
01	AG3EH850	Battery, wet	12	1	23	10	3
01	HD12	Battery Fluid	10	0	8	4	0
01	M2484	Battery, wet	12	54	216	139	10

End of list

One option is to run the report with the on-order amount added to the on-hand amount when calculating the days supply. With this modification we will isolate *only* items where we are in trouble even after allowing for the on-order quantities.

The Hot List Report enables the manager to quickly see how the inventory of any particular vendor is shaping up. Note how much more effective this report is compared to a simple "out of stock" report which gives feedback when the problem is already too far gone.

There are many uses for the Hot List. One application is to run the hot list just prior to building an order for a specific vendor. Depending on which items are beginning to look problematic, the purchasing manager will know whether to force the order to meet an economic break point or whether to hold out for another day or two to see if the load will fill out on its own.

Another application is to run the report twice a week on the major products of the company as an exception report for the outside salespeople. If an item is not on the report, the salespeople can assume the product is in stock since the report only lists items that have a ten-day supply or less on hand. If the item is on the report, the salespeople need to call in to verify availability because, although the report indicates some product is available, it is not a sufficient quantity to assure that the supply will hold.

Finally, the Hot List Report provides the General Manager with an early indication of the health of the inventory. If this list suddenly starts to grow, it is an excellent early warning that a problem is starting to develop.

Evaluating Special Buys

In many industries, vendors offer special "one time" buys. For example, a vendor may come in and say, "We will give you 10 percent off any purchases you make this month for the following three items." The challenge for the buyer, then, is to trigger a purchase order for the right amount of each SKU so that the savings are maximized when the cost of carrying the excess inventory is comprehended.

This type of ordering decision is generally made by "gut feel," since the numerical calculations are highly complex. It is possible, however, to use the demand forecasting system to mathematically arrive at the optimum solution.

10.1   **The Calculation Methodology**

Conceptionally, the calculation can be described as follows:

The first component of the calculation is the savings. This is the dollar amount of product being purchased in excess of the normal reorder amount, multiplied by the discount being offered. It is represented by the straight line on the following graph (Exhibit 0). The more you buy, the more you save.

The cost side of the equation is made up of a number of components. First we have to determine the "extra" months supply of product that will be layered in as a result of the extra buy. This will be comprised of: the initial amount of product on hand or on order (since we are adding the new product on top of this layer), plus the months supply of new product being added. We then have to back out of this figure the months supply represented by the safety stock (since theoretically this stock is a built-in layer and will never be used) plus the months supply represented by the lead time (since the product will not even arrive until after the lead time).

The added cost of the buy is the resulting "extra months supply" multiplied by the value of the extra product, times the percent carrying cost for inventory.

The cost equation is represented by the upward curving line on the following graph. The line curves upward because each additional unit purchased creates a layer that causes the next unit to stay in the inventory that much longer.

The net cost of the transaction is the sum of the savings less the extra inventory carrying cost, which is represented by the dome-shaped curve on the graph.

Exhibit O

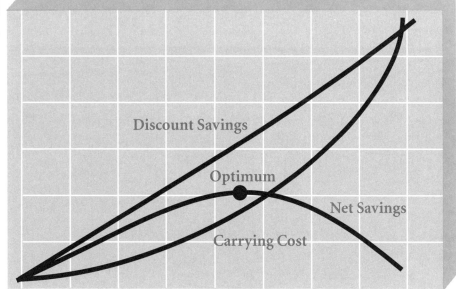

Extra Units

Note: As the number of extra units purchased increases, the savings increase, but at a diminishing rate. Eventually the carrying cost overwhelms the initial savings and the savings "top out" and start down. The optimum point, therefore, is at the crest of the curve. The next unit purchased after the crest of the curve will utilize its entire savings in carrying cost by the time it is sold.

The Actual Calculations

The specific calculations for evaluating special buys are as follows:

Assume the following:

FCST	=	Forecast in units per month
OH	=	On-hand balance
OO	=	On-order amount
N	=	Normal order amount being suggested by the system
Z	=	Total of the above three items
PI	=	Cost of carrying inventory in percent/month
PC	=	Percent discount being offered
C	=	Product cost
SS	=	Safety stock expressed as months supply
L	=	Lead time in months
Q	=	The "extra quantity" we are trying to determine

Then:

Savings = SV = C x Q x PC

Months supply being added =
MS = (Z/FCST) + (.5 x Q)/FCST + SS + L
Expense = EX = MS x PI x C x Q

Net Savings = SV - EX

The only unusual part of the equation relates to the 0.5 multiplier of Q in the months supply calculation. The rationale is as follows: During the period that the Q is being consumed, it will exist an average of half the amount (i.e., it starts at the full amount and ends at zero).

We must solve the equation for Q at the point where Net Savings is at a maximum. This is accomplished by taking the differential of the equation and setting it equal to zero, and then solving for Q.

This determination is possible by this method because the differential of an equation is the rate of change of the curve (or the slope of the line that is tangent to the curve). Consequently we want to calculate the point at which this slope is zero (i.e., the tangent is parallel to the X axis). This, by definition, is the optimum — or highest point — to which the curve can rise.

The actual mathematics are as follows:

The full equation for net savings is:

Net Savings=   **SV - EX**

Net Savings =   (Q x C x PC)

                 - (Z/FCST + .5 x Q/FCST - SS - L) x PI x C x Q

                 = Q x C x PC - PI x C x Q x (Z/FCST)

                 - PI x C x (.5 x Q^2/FCST) + SS x PI x C x Q + L x PI x C x Q

The differential of this equation is:

                 = C x PC - PI x C x (Z/FCST) - (2 x Q x .5 x C x PI)/FCST

                 + SS x PI x C + L x PI x C

Setting this equation to zero allows us to immediately cancel all the "C" terms (which illustrates why the product cost is irrelevant).

                 0.0 = PC - PI x Z/FCST - 1.0 x PI x Q/FCST + SS x PI + L x PI

Solving for Q:

                 Q x PI/FCST = PC - PI x Z/FCST + SS x PI + L x PI

The final equation that results from this mathematical process is:

                 Q = FCST x (PC/PI - Z/FCST + SS + L)

Note: The forecast used by the system is for the two months ahead of the current month. This is a compromise, since we cannot truly simulate the usage over the period in question, and we do not know the length of that period until we have the solution. It's a mathematical Catch 22.

By going out two months, we at least roughly comprehend the period of concern and avoid the trap of bringing in product as the strong season is drawing to a close.

10.3 The Actual Screen Sequence

The procedure for working a "special buys" feature into the ordering sequence is as follows:

a. During the ordering process, move the highlighter to the SKU in question. Hit the appropriate function key and have a screen appear with the following prompt:

Percent Discount being offered ? _____

b. Enter the discount.

c. Hit the enter key and have following screen appear:

Item: Z24LTHD5
Optimum Purchase Quantity for Special Buy

Extra Units	Savings	Expense	Net Savings
66	$203	$146	$57

"Normal Order"	17
Total Order	83

Accept Recommendation?____Yes____

d. By hitting the "Y" key, the reorder screen will reappear; if you elected to accept the order recommendation, the new numbers will appear in the SUGG column for that SKU.

Note: While using this system, a purchasing manager could negotiate directly with a vendor who was either physically present or on the phone. With the ability to try out different discount levels and know their financial implications, a manager could seek the optimum return for the company under various scenarios.

Let me reiterate something we covered earlier. You do not have to understand the mathematics behind a complex determination to use the system, any more than you need to understand advanced electronics to make a telephone call. The mathematics used to arrive at this discount screen are — I believe you will agree — rather formidable. Yet, in the end, the complex calculations result in a screen display which is extremely easy to understand, interpret, and — most important — use.

10.4 An Observation About the Size of the Recommended Order

You may be surprised, as I was, by the quantities the system wants you to order to optimize the discount being offered by the vendor. It turns out that if the cost of carrying inventory is only 1.5 percent per month, and the discount being offered is for example 6 percent, you can carry a lot of inventory to enjoy the maximum savings from the discount.

If you are nervous about ordering the large amounts of product the system is recommending, you can increase the carrying cost percentage or drop back to an artificially lower discount level and trigger that amount.

Frankly, I had a real problem with my first use of the system, and cut the order quantities back as I have just suggested. Nevertheless, the system pushed me into much higher levels of purchases than I would have intuitively executed. Consequently, we capitalized on the vendor's discount to a higher degree than I would have on my own.

My resulting order was in excellent proportion to the expected demand, so we ended up with stock that was purchased at a good discount, and an inventory that was in balance. This is in contrast to the typical situation where the purchasing manager ends up ordering "a pallet of this, two pallets of that, etc." In fact, the demand forecasting system may not order any of an SKU if the amount on hand from prior actions makes the new discount opportunity worthless.

We have dealt with the situation where there was an opportunity to buy added quantities of a specific SKU or group of SKUs at a discount. Another situation you might encounter is when a vendor offers a discount on an entire product line (e.g., any order shipped this month will carry an extra eight percent discount).

A variation of this situation is when a price increase has been announced for an entire product line, but there is still an opportunity to place an order to avoid the price increase. If you think about it, a discount on a coming price increase you wish to avoid is exactly the same as a one-time discount. When this discount offer arises, with it comes the classic dilemma of just how large an order to place to capitalize on the current lower price while at the same time keeping the carrying cost of the added inventory to a minimum.

All the logic discussed in Section 10.0 is applicable to this blanket discount situation; however, the process now applies to each and every SKU for that vendor. In fact, we could build an order on the vendor by using the techniques discussed in Section 10.0 and stepping through each SKU one at a time.

However, we can utilize the demand forecasting system to simplify this task. After calling up the reorder screen and hitting an appropriate function key, we can have the system prompt us for the amount of the discount being offered (or the amount of the coming price increase). After we enter the appropriate percentage, the system can then go through the process discussed in Section 10.0, and place the optimum order amount in the SUGG column for each and every SKU

At this point we are still in a position to interact with the system to override specific recommendations and to interject any special information we may possess.

The techniques we have been discussing in the last few sections are powerful and unique. The demand forecasting system will take you far beyond the typical "best guess" methods you have had to utilize in the past and provide you with optimum guidance in order building.

There is one variation on the impending price increase situation that the system will not comprehend. In our business — and I'm sure in yours — it is not uncommon to place a large order when a price increase is announced. However, it sometimes happens that as soon as the product arrives, it is apparent that the price increase is not going to hold, and we now have added product in inventory with no economic offset. You are on you own on this one!

Reordering at Two Levels of Lead Times

You may be faced with a special situation which does not fit into the reordering approach we have covered up to this point. For example, at Battery and Tire Warehouse, once every six weeks we place an order with an overseas manufacturer for a full sea-container of tires that has a delivery lead time of almost three months. If there were no other considerations, demand forecasting would handle this reordering situation routinely, despite the long lead times and infrequent reordering cycle.

Between container receipts, however, the manufacturer allows us to order directly from its domestic warehouse in smaller quantities and with fast delivery of one week. We are limited on the amount of "fill-in orders" we can execute, and we keep track of that limitation externally.

If we were to handle the large container orders conventionally and put the on-order amounts directly into the system, the system would fail to take advantage of the fill-in reordering opportunities. The system would see the large on-order quantity and not call for product, even though a particular SKU was being drawn down at a faster-than-expected rate.

We can solve this problem quite simply, and even further drive the fill-in opportunity to our advantage. To generate the container order, set the lead time and order frequency information at their proper levels. Then generate the container order in the normal manner. At this point, instead of fully executing the purchase order (which would place the quantities ordered into the on-order field), place the purchase order into a "holding" stage.

Next, set the lead times and order frequency to the levels consistent with the domestic warehouse fill-in process, and trigger fill-in orders at their appropriate times. The system will then order only product needed to protect for the time horizon dictated by the fill-in order cycle. (It most likely will not want product for quite a while after a container has arrived.)

When the next container is due to arrive within the lead time of the fill-in order, load the container order into the on-order status (i.e., if the lead time for the domestic warehouse is one week, load in the container on-order status a week before it is due to arrive). The system will note that product is about to arrive and will not order fill-in product improperly. After the container arrives, repeat the sequence all over again.

While our example deals with an overseas container shipment situation, many analogous situations can arise that pose the same problems. They all can be handled with the same logic.

One of the classic challenges in scheduling a factory, with or without an MRP (Material Requirement Planning) system, is developing a decent master schedule to drive the production. If the factory "produces to order," this is not a problem since the schedule is the actual order book.

A more typical situation, however, requires that the factory produce to some sort of an inventory level that may be used to provide faster customer service or to buffer the plant against periodic volume fluctuations, or both.

The demand forecasting system is ideal to satisfy the need for scheduling in the manufacturing industry. In this application, the "vendor" is the factory. All the parameters used in the demand forecasting system have manufacturing parallels:

a. **Lead Time** — This becomes the length of time from the longest lead time for raw material to the final availability of the finished product. Note, however, that it is necessary to set the lead time to this extended level only when you are looking for a high immediate fill level directly from inventory.

    Frequently, the only objective is to shorten the normal manufacturing lead time. In this case, the lead time can be set to an artificially lower level, and the system can run on a "starved basis." The system will trigger a product requirement that will start the production process, but before the product is actually completed, the orders will arrive for delivery right off the line, but with a shortened lead time.

    I was on a consulting assignment where we installed exactly this concept. The normal lead time for this industry was six weeks from order placement to delivery. By driving the production schedule with our system, and by setting the lead time at an artificially low level of three weeks, we were able to offer three-week delivery promises with virtually no inventory accumulation.

b. **Order Frequency** — This becomes the production scheduling cycle, which most likely is weekly, but could be any measure of time. The resulting order, if the frequency is weekly, is for one week. The MRP system slots the various production aspects of that order into the appropriate "buckets."

c. **Safety Factor** — If the objective is to supply directly from inventory, then the safety factor has the same definition it had in a normal inventory situation (e.g., 95 percent means that we would like to provide 95 percent fill rates to our customers directly from our stock).

If we are running the system "starved," with an artificially low lead time, we begin to cloud the safety stock picture. The shortened lead time and the safety factor interact to interfere with the definition of safety stock. In this situation, I recommend that you use a safety factor of 80 percent so some safety stock is still being generated, but less than in a classic inventory situation.

d. **Pallet Size, Lot Sensitivity, and EOQ** can be utilized to drive the "run size" of the production schedule. There are perfect parallels between the EOQ or pallets and a production run of a particular product. The pallet feature can be used if the run lengths are fairly firm, and the EOQ feature can be used if the economic trade-offs are more subtle. In using the EOQ feature, handling cost becomes the set-up costs, and carrying costs remain the same. All the same concepts then apply.

In Section 6.0, we discussed the EOQ concept and how it comprehends the trade-off between the cost of handling and stocking a product versus the cost of carrying extra inventory. In certain circumstances, an additional EOQ consideration is driven by the fact that the vendor has set price breaks at different quantity points for each SKU.

This situation can arise when the vendor custom produces the product and has to consider the set-up cost for making the item. For example, a single item may be priced at 95 cents, 50 cents if purchased in amounts of 100 or more, and 35 cents if purchased in amounts over 300. This type of pricing can be dictated by packaging considerations as well.

Using this set of circumstances, let's assume the system triggers a reorder for 65 items. At this level our unit price would be 95 cents, and it's obvious that we should consider buying 100 to get the 50-cent price — or even 300 to get the 35-cent price. It is by no means obvious, however, exactly where the optimum level lies.

We can add a feature to the demand forecasting system that will handle these considerations with great accuracy and consistency:

1. Determine the amount of product desired by the normal "Reorder Target" calculation.

2. Test each of the next price breaks to determine whether the cost of carrying the extra product is offset by the price discount.

    The mathematics for this determination are very straightforward. At each next higher level of purchase, have the system calculate the price savings for the entire purchase, which is the difference between the two price levels, times the units involved. Then determine the added number of months of "unwanted" inventory the new volume creates, and figure the carrying cost of the added product. Then divide this figure in half since the "average" time the product will sit around is half of the total. Note: Use the inventory carrying cost percentage as we did in the previous EOQ calculations in Section 5.4.1.2.

3. When the cost of carrying the extra inventory is greater than the savings by going to the next higher price break, we know that the prior level of consideration was the optimum purchasing quantity.

To incorporate the quantity price break feature, it is necessary to have additional data fields in each SKU record to carry the price break information. It takes two fields for each price break level. In our example, we would need four fields to indicate the new costs (50 cents and 35 cents) at each of the two volume levels (100 and 300).

Once the feature is built in, the system will automatically engage this new option when building an order. It will check the volume trade-offs while it simultaneously deals with all other issues discussed earlier, such as full truckload requirements, seasonality, trends, etc. It is staggering to consider the potential savings the demand forecasting system will provide in a purchasing environment when compared to an approach that attempts to manually cope with all variables.

Many companies operate with one or more central warehouses which not only ship direct to customers, but also restock a series of satellite warehouses. These central warehouses are frequently referred to as "mixing warehouses" because they allow for economical receipt of large shipments from a wide variety of vendors. At the central warehouse, products from all vendors are then available to be shipped "mixed" to the satellite warehouses.

Warehouses interact with other warehouses in endless variations, but they all are susceptible to being restocked in an extremely effective way using the tools of the demand forecasting system.

Restocking a central warehouse is done in the classic manner, with the various suppliers being called up for analysis at their appropriate times. All the issues of order frequency and lead time discussed earlier are appropriate. The only difference is that the "sales history" that drives the forecast for each item is the total of all direct customer shipments *plus all transfers to the satellite warehouses.* This does, after all, constitute the shipment experience of the central warehouse in fulfilling its obligations to both direct customers and the satellite warehouses that are dependent on it for product availability.

Restocking the satellite warehouse is another story. In this case, the "vendor" is the central warehouse, since the central warehouse is supplying the satellites with full product lines from all vendors. "Order frequency" is the time period between shipments from the central point to the satellites. Typically this would be weekly. "Lead time" is the full span from the time of initiating the order to when it is available for shipment to the customer — not just the time it takes in shipping.

There is one additional caveat regarding warehouse stock. You may be willing to give much less than 97 percent fill out of the satellite warehouse on the basis that replenishment is so frequent. In this case, it is a matter of setting the fill rate expectancy to a lower number, such as 90 percent, and letting the system take down the safety stock accordingly. As I have stated before, it is prudent to "play" with this process rather than assume that all these figures are gospel. Start at 95 percent and then drop the percentage carefully over time — and see how it looks.

There are some theories that suggest that a different system should be used for satellite versus central warehouses. Frankly, I feel these concepts arise out of past practices that were flawed at a fundamental level. In my opinion, you can apply the demand forecasting concepts we have developed to both classes of warehouses with no special changes other than properly defining sales flow and vendor.

The only exception to this rule is satellites that are so small as to be trivial. In this case, some form of periodically reviewed "model stock" may be in order. It's not that demand forecasting will not work — it's simply a case of shooting a mouse with an elephant gun.

Early in this book, I recommended a forecasting method (Exponential Averaging) which is far superior to any other method of forecasting I have encountered. This forecasting method has been used in the business environment, and specifically in inventory management, for a considerable period of time with great success.

Actually, most forecasting techniques can claim success if they have replaced some simplistic system, particularly the highly common method of "eyeballing" the historic data. Virtually any quantitative disciplined forecasting method will yield some measure of improvement. The real issue is which system, in the final analysis, will consistently do the best job.

As you explore ways to maximize your inventory performance, you will encounter many other forecasting systems which claim to be superior. But, beware! There are pitfalls to them all. One such forecasting system simultaneously maintains a wide variety of forecasts for the same SKU. It utilizes a mix of these methods:

- **Simple exponential smoothing (but maintaining a number of different forecasts, each with a different alpha level)**

- **Second degree exponential smoothing (extrapolating a trend if it appears to be developing)**

- **Different techniques of dealing with seasonality**

- **Moving averages (using different numbers of months)**

- **An average of the past years months, or group of months**

In this multiple forecasting approach, the system determines which of the forecasting techniques has been doing the best historic job of forecasting for that particular SKU (based on some measure of past error levels). The system then uses that forecast technique for the next forecast.

While this approach has a certain amount of initial appeal, it is a lot of processing for no return and, in fact, has the potential to do more harm than good.

The following metaphor provides some idea of why the concept is flawed. Assume for a minute that you are in a situation where it is absolutely vital that you flip a coin and have it come up heads. (Heads and you get a million dollars, tails and they cut off your right ear.) To improve your odds, you gather a group of people in a room and have them start flipping coins. After a period of time, you pick the person who has the best ratio of heads to tails, and you take that person into the final toss.

I believe you will agree that this approach does nothing to improve your odds, since the person you selected had a better ratio of heads to tails due strictly to random chance, and the odds on the next flip will be fifty-fifty regardless of the person's track record.

Since the forecasting situation is more complex, the proponents of multiple forecasting methods would argue that in contrast to an individual's coin tossing skills, one forecast may truly be superior to another. The idea that one forecast is better for one SKU, and another forecast is better for a different SKU, raises my eyebrow, however. An even more serious concern of mine is the fact that the chosen forecast could be the worst one for that situation at the moment. Consider the following example:

Let's assume a product has a fundamental cyclical nature. A second degree exponential average, which handles trends very well, will comfortably match the sales history of this product for the period of time when the item is on its upward trend. Unfortunately, when the item reaches its peak and starts heading downward, the forecast will actually predict the opposite, and be way off on the high side, bringing in excess inventory at the very time it is not needed.

In fact, the multiple forecast concept will be notoriously flawed in all "turning point" examples since, by definition, it will rely on prior patterns of demand.

This is only one example of how a forecasting approach can fail to consider product characteristics or market circumstances. For the few times the multiple forecasting technique will enhance the forecast, it will just as often hurt the forecast. The benefits will be modest, whereas the times we are misled will tend to be substantial. We can live with modest errors, but major blunders will sink the system —not only in reality, but even more important, in the minds of the purchasing managers.

It is my hope that by now many of the inventory management techniques I have presented are looking very feasible for your operations. If I have been successful, you should see area after area that can benefit from the management tools and computer programs we have discussed. Let's face it, unless something tangible happens, the whole exercise is merely academic.

To translate theory into action takes some fundamental management actions. The top person and key managers in your organization must provide leadership and direction. Inventory management is not an area where you can "put out the dish and see if the cat eats it." Your business is at stake. The profit vise is tightening all the time. If your business has yet to feel the full impact, you are lucky — not because it won't happen, but because you have additional time to take action.

In order to make the transition into computer-aided inventory management, you will have to install the best systems and concepts for the job. In doing so, you will have to be sensitive to the skill levels of your existing work force and to the culture of the organization — but not to the point of inaction. Everyone will have to make some changes, not the least of whom may be you.

On the bright side, however, you and your employees will learn new skills and become more effective in your respective professions. You will be part of a company that is smooth running, well managed, more profitable, and a more exciting place to work. In this new work environment, the computer will be doing 98 percent of the "dog work" while you and your employees will be exercising unique human judgment to maximize the resources of the business.

At Battery and Tire Warehouse, we are doing 250 percent more sales per office employee than when I acquired the business nine years ago. This didn't happen by working harder, it happened by working smarter — backed by systems, systems, and more systems.

I wish you the same and even greater success!

Glossary of Terms

Alpha Level

A multiplier that sets the responsiveness of the Exponential Average to new data. Usually stated as .2, .3, or .4. The higher the number, the more responsive the average. I strongly recommend using .3 as a good compromise between responsiveness and stability.

Basic Coverage

Sufficient stock to cover the period of exposure dictated by the order frequency and the lead time. If the forecast is perfect, this amount of product will insure 100 percent fill of orders. Basic Coverage is one segment of the Reorder Target calculation; Safety Stock is the other part.

Cost of Initiating and Handling an Order

The incremental (out-of-pocket) cost in dollars to initiate an order for a specific SKU and to receive and put the product into inventory. Referred to as "C" in the EOQ calculation.

Deseasonalized Exponential Average

The Exponential Average of the sales history of a product, with the seasonal characteristics removed. When this average is multiplied by the Seasonal Index, it provides the forecast for the coming months.

EOQ

Economic Order Quantity. An override of the normal replenishment amount when it makes good economic sense to bring in extra product to offset the need to reorder again shortly. The figure is a tradeoff between the cost of handling a product and putting it into stock and the carrying cost of having inventory on hand.

Exponential Average

The forecasting technique I recommended to drive the Demand Forecasting System. It is fundamentally the same as a Moving Average, except that each month is weighted by an ever-decreasing amount, with the first month being the heaviest. As each month of data becomes older, its weighing in the calculation for the new forecast goes down.

Filter

A device that guards the forecast from being wrongly influenced by "wild" sales levels that are one-time events. If a new point of sales history is above the range of normal variation, the filter simply knocks the point down to the outer range of normal and uses that number to update the average.

Flag

A single letter that appears on the far right side of the main ordering screen to alert the user to the fact that the reorder amount recommended by the system has been overridden.

Goal Seeking

A technique used to artificially inflate the normal reorder amount to reach a given total quantity. (e.g., If the normal reorder is 36,000 pounds, but we need 40,000 pounds to met the vendor's requirement for a full truckload, then by using the Goal Seeking feature and selecting weight as the criterion on which to drive, the system will inflate the original order to optimally arrive at the amount of product to order and still be at 40,000 pounds.)

HIGH

One of the four statistically based order levels used to determine reorder amounts. HIGH is one level higher than the NORM.

Hot List

An exception report that highlights products that are dangerously low in their days of supply and could possibly go out of stock before a replenishment arrives.

LOW

One of the four statistically based order levels used to determine reorder amounts. LOW is one level lower than the NORM.

MAD

Mean Average Deviation. A measurement of the variability of the sales history for a particular item. The higher the number (relative to its average), the less predicable the item will be. This figure is a key component of the Safety Stock. It is also used to establish the range for the Filter.

MAX

One of the four statistically based order levels used to determine reorder amounts. MAX is two levels higher than the NORM.

NORM

The amount of product the system is recommending be reordered. It is the difference between the Net Available and the Target.

Moving Average

A simplistic forecasting method used by many inventory systems. It is calculated by adding a specific number of months of history together and then dividing by the number of months used.

Percent Fill

A percentage that indicates how effectively the inventory is satisfying customer demand for products on the Authorized Stock List. It can be calculated in different ways, but the classic approach is to note the number of orders that were satisfied directly from on-hand inventory. (e.g., 95 percent fill would indicate that 95 percent of product orders were filled directly from stock with no delays.)

Pipeline

This term refers to the whereabouts of product that is on order but has not yet been received. When a product is "in the pipeline," the order has been placed and the product will arrive at some future date, but the product is not yet in your inventory and, therefore, it is not costing you anything.

Reorder Target

This number drives the Demand Forecasting System. It is a calculation that comprehends the amount of stock required to cover the period of exposure dictated by the order frequency and the lead time, plus the amount of stock needed to compensate for the inherent inaccuracy of the forecast. The reorder amount is the difference between the Reorder Target and the amount currently on hand or in the pipeline.

Safety Factor

A number used in the Safety Stock calculation to determine the amount of extra stock needed to compensate for the inaccuracy of the forecast. It is statistically arrived at after fill rates are established.

Safety Stock

The amount of stock needed to compensate for the inaccuracy of the forecast. The two parameters that drive this figure are the MAD (which is the measure of the forecast inaccuracy) and the Safety Factor (which is derived from the desired fill rate). Safety Stock is one-half of the Reorder Target calculation; Basic Coverage is the other half.

Seasonality

The degree to which an SKU responds to seasonal influences.

Seasonal Index

An index number (usually expressed as a single digit plus a single decimal point — 1.2, 1.0, 0.9) which represents the degree to which product demand for the month varies from the NORM due to seasonality. A Seasonal Index of .8, for example, indicates that in that specific month, the demand for the product will be roughly 20 percent below the NORM.

SKU

Stock Keeping Unit. Each SKU represents a specific product or product group that must carry its own stock number to differentiate it in inventory. All products that can be co-mingled in inventory will carry the same SKU. When products cannot be co-mingled, they must have their own stock numbers. For example, if a number of products are identical in every way, and the customer doesn't care who the manufacturer is, then all these products can carry the same stock number and will constitute a single SKU. If, however, the customer cares that these products come from different manufacturers, then each of these products will need a separate stock number, and we will have a number of SKUs.